Middle Level ISEE®

MATH

Larchmont Academics

LarchmontAcademics.com

1

To request permissions or inquire about buying this title in bulk, contact the publisher at theiseeacademy@gmail.com.

ISBN: 9798549306868

Second paperback edition November 2022.

ISEE® is a registered trademark of the Educational Records Bureau, which was not involved in the production of, and does not endorse, sponsor, or certify this product.

Neither the author or publisher claim any responsibility for the accuracy and appropriateness of the content in this book, nor do they claim any responsibility over the outcome of students who use these materials.

Published in the USA

Larchmont Academics
Los Angeles, CA

LarchmontAcademics.com

TABLE OF CONTENTS

Preparing for the Test

What to Expect on the ISEE®

The ISEE® has two math sections: Quantitative Reasoning and Mathematics Achievement. This book will prepare you for both sections.

Quantitative Reasoning tests your ability to use what you know to solve thinking problems.

Type of Question	Number of Questions
Word Problems	18-21
Quantitative Comparisons	14-17
Total Questions	37

*5 questions are experimental and are not scored

You have 35 minutes for this section.

Mathematics Achievement tests your level of mastery of math skills.

Type of Question	Number of Questions
Whole Numbers	7 - 10
Decimals, Percents, Fractions	7 – 10
Algebraic Concepts	9 - 13
Geometry	4 - 6
Measurement	4 - 6
Data and Probability	5 - 9
Total Questions	47

*5 questions are experimental and are not scored

You have 40 minutes for this section.

This book combines both sections as they require an understanding of similar skills. On the test, you can expect certain types of problems and this book will help you learn to solve them.

Question Format

 ## Classic Multiple Choice

You will be asked a question and then choose from 4 options (A, B, C or D)

Which questions are like this?
About half of the Quantitative Reasoning questions and all of the Mathematics Achievement Questions.

Example:
What is the sum of 4x and 3x?
(A) 12x
(B) 6x
(C) 3+4x
(D) 7x

The answer would be D because 3x + 4x = 7x

Quantitative Comparisons

You will be given two items (either numbers or problems) and asked to decide which is greater, if they are equal, or if it cannot be determined.

Which questions are like this?
About half of the Quantitative Reasoning questions and none of the Mathematics Achievement questions.

Example:

Column A   Column B
0.25 $\frac{1}{4}$

(A) Column A is greater

(B) Column B is greater

(C) Column A and Column B are equal

(D) The relationship cannot be determined with the information given

The answer would be C because 0.25 = ¼

Timing Strategies

Keep Track of Your Timing

Quantitative Reasoning

37 Questions – 35 Minutes

You have just under 1 minute per question.

Do your best to finish the word problems by the 20-minute mark!

Mathematics Achievement

47 Questions – 40 Minutes

You have 50 seconds per question.

Do your best to finish question 24 by the 20-minute mark!

Know when to guess and move on!

When should you guess and plan to come back if you have time at the end?

If you think it will take more than 2 minutes

If the content looks completely new to you

Common Tricky Question Types

 ## Be ready for common tricky question types!

There are many types of questions that frequently appear on the test. Some may seem tricky at first, but if you know how to solve them, they are not so hard. You may just need to know how the test is trying to trick you or a quick fact to help you solve them.

Throughout the book, look for this symbol, , to practice with a common tricky question type.

ISEE Scoring

 ## Scoring the Mathematics Achievement Section

The ISEE scoring process has a few steps. It starts with your **raw score** which is based on the number of questions you answered correctly. This is then converted into a **scaled score** which is accompanied by a **percentile rank**. This percentile represents how you compare to other test takers. So, if you are in the 89th percentile, this does not mean you answered 89 percent of questions correctly. Instead, it means scored higher than 89 percent of test-takers. Your percentile score is then converted into a **stanine score** with a scale marked from 1 to 9 (9 being the highest.)

Percentile ———Stanine

1-3 ——— 1
4-10——2
11-22——3
23-39——4
40-59——5
60-76——6
77-88——7
89-95——8
96-99——9

Arithmetic

Order of Operations

What do I need to know?

Follow this order whenever you do a math problem with multiple steps.

1. Parenthesis and grouping symbols

2. Exponents

3. Multiplication and Division from left to right

4. Addition and Subtraction from left to right

How do I remember?

Remember the acronym PEMDAS or...

P

E

$\overrightarrow{MD}$

$\overrightarrow{AS}$

Example: 5 + 3 x 4 – (2 + 2)

1. Parenthesis and grouping symbols	5 + 3 x 4 – (2 + 2) 5 + 3 x 4 – 4
2. Exponents	None
6 Multiplication and Division from left to right	5 + 3 x 4 – 4 5 + 12 – 4
7 Addition and Subtraction from left to right	5 + 12 – 4 17 – 4 17 – 4 ⑬

1. $4 + 2 \times 3 - (3 + 4)$

   (A) 3

   (B) 4

   (C) 8

   (D) 11

2. $2(16 - 3 \times 4) + 2 \times 3$

   (A) 12

   (B) 14

   (C) 102

   (D) 110

3. $3 \times 4 - 2 \times 4 + 3$

   (A) 5

   (B) 7

   (C) 27

   (D) 43

4. $4^2 + 5 - (2 \times 4) \times 2$

   (A) 5

   (B) 10

   (C) 16

   (D) 26

5. $4(3 + 5) - 3 \times 2$

   (A) 20

   (B) 24

   (C) 26

   (D) 58

6. $7 - 8 + (9 - 6 \div 3) \times 2$

   (A) 9

   (B) 13

   (C) 7

   (D) 12

7. $4 \times 8 \div 16 - 3 + 1$

   (A) -2

   (B) 0

   (C) 4

   (D) 3

8. $(-10 - 2 \times 6 \div 3) + 5^2$

   (A) -9

   (B) 10

   (C) 11

   (D) -12

9. $7(7 \times 2 - 9) \div 5$

   (A) 7

   (B) 5

   (C) -1

   (D) 10

10. $(7 \times 7 - 25) \div 8 \times 2 - 7$

   (A) 0

   (B) -3

   (C) 4

   (D) -1

Order of Operations - Answers and Explanations

1. The correct answer is 'A'

4 + 2 x 3 - (7)

4 + 6 - 7

10 - 7

3

2. The correct answer is 'B'

$2(16 - 3 \times 4) + 2 \times 3$

2 (16 - 12) + 2 x 3

2 (4) + 6

8 + 6

14

3. The correct answer is 'B'

3 x 4 - 2 x 4 + 3

12 - 8 + 3

4 + 3

7

4. The correct answer is 'A'

$4^2 + 5 - (2 \times 4) \times 2$

16 + 5 - (8) x 2

16 + 5 - 16

21-16

5

5. The correct answer is 'C'

$4(3 + 5) - 3 \times 2$

4 (8) - 3 x 2

32 - 6

26

6. The correct answer is 'B'

7-8+(9-2)×2

7-8+7×2

7-8+14

-1+14=13

7. The correct answer is 'B'

$4 \times (1 \div 2) - 3 + 1$

2-3+1

-1+1

0

8. The correct answer is 'C'

$(-10 - 2 \times 2) + 5^2$

$(-10 - 4) + 5^2$

-14 + 25

11

9. The correct answer is 'A'

$7(14 - 9) \div 5$

$7(5) \div 5$

$35 \div 5$

7

10. The correct answer is 'D'

$(49 - 25) \div 8 \times 2 - 7$

$24 \div 8 \times 2 - 7$

$3 \times 2 - 7$

$6 - 7 = -1$

Factors

What do I need to know?

Vocabulary Term	Definition	Example
Factors	The whole numbers that can be multiplied to get the target number	The factors of 10 are 1, 10, 2, and 5.
Greatest Common Factor (GCF)	The largest factor of two different numbers.	10 and 15 both have the factors 1 and 5. The GCF is 5.
Least Common Multiple (LCM)	The smallest number that two other numbers can be multiplied into. This is usually used in finding a common denominator.	6 and 9 both can be multiplied up to 18. Their Least common multiple is 18.
Prime Numbers	A number that can only be divided by 1 and itself	5 is prime because the only factors are 1 and 5.

 How can I tell which number is prime?

Remember: A number that is prime is ONLY divisible by 1 and itself.

1. **Does it end in an even number or a 5?**

   If so, it is NOT prime since it is divisible by 2 or 5.

2. **Add up all of the digits. Is the answer divisible by 3?**

   If so, it is NOT prime. You can tell if a number is divisible by 3 because the sum of the digits will also be divisible by 3.

3. **If you are still deciding between two numbers, try dividing by 7 or 11.**

   This will give you an answer on the ISEE

Example: Which of the following numbers is prime?

(A) 438

(B) 263

(C) 365

(D) 483

1. Does it end in an even number or a 5?

   (A) 438

   (B) 263

   (C) 365

   (D) 483

2. Add up all of the digits. Is the answer divisible by 3?

   (B) 263

   2 + 6 + 3 = 11

   263 is NOT divisible by 3

   (D) 483

   4 + 8 + 3 = 15

   483 is divisible by 3

So, the answer is 263 because all of the other numbers are divisible by either 2, 3 or 5.

   (A) 438

   (B) 263

   (C) 365

   (D) 483

Factors

---

1. Which of the following numbers is prime?

   (A) 546

   (B) 330

   (C) 417

   (D) 313

2. What is the greatest common factor of 18 and 42?

   (A) 6

   (B) 9

   (C) 7

   (D) 18

3. What is the least common multiple of 14 and 6?

   (A) 28

   (B) 42

   (C) 84

   (D) 2

4. Which of the following numbers is divisible by 6?

   (Hint: A number that is divisible by 6 is also divisible by 2 and 3)

   (A) 269

   (B) 266

   (C) 252

   (D) 345

5. Which of the following numbers is a factor of 343?

   (A) 3

   (B) 5

   (C) 2

   (D) 7

6. Which of the following is the greatest common factor of 30 and 24?

   (A) 2

   (B) 3

   (C) 5

   (D) 6

7. Which of the following numbers is prime?

   (A) 942

   (B) 947

   (C) 945

   (D) 948

8. What is the product of the greatest common factor of 2 and 3 and the least common multiple of 2 and 3?

   (A) 1

   (B) 2

   (C) 3

   (D) 6

9. How many prime numbers are there between 1 and 10? (Remember 1 is neither prime nor composite.)

(A) 4

(B) 3

(C) 5

(D) 6

10. What is the least common multiple of 8 and 12?

(A) 16

(B) 32

(C) 24

(D) 8

Factors - Answers and Explanations

1. The correct answer is 'D'

546 and 330 are both even, so they are not prime.

The digits of 417 add up to 12 which is divisible by three, so 417 is also divisible by 3 and not prime.

313 is the only option left. It is also odd and not divisible by 3, 5 or 7.

2. The correct answer is 'A'

Start with 18. The high factors of 18 are 18, 9, and 6.

18 and 9 do not go into 42 but 6 does. So, 6 is the answer.

3. The correct answer is 'B'

Start with the higher number:

Multiples of 14: 28, 42

42/6 is 7, so 42 is correct. 6 does not go into 14 or 28.

4. The correct answer is 'C'

Since a number that is divisible by 6 is also divisible by 3 and 2, eliminate all of the odd number answer choices. Now, add up the digits of the remaining choices:

2+5+2= 9

2+6+6= 14

So, 252 is correct

5. The correct answer is 'D'

NOT 3: 3+4+3 = 10 which is not divisible by 3

NOT 5: Does not end in a 5

NOT 2: It is not even

7 is correct

6. The correct answer is 'D'

2, 3, 5, and 6 are all factors of 30. 2, 3, and 6 are all factors of 24. 6 is the greatest factor.

7. The correct answer is 'B'

942 and 948 end with even numbers. So they are divisible by 2. 945 ends with 5. So, it is divisible by 5. 947 is the only option left and is prime.

8. The correct answer is 'D'

The greatest common factor of 2 and 3 is 1. The least common multiple of 2 and 3 is 6. The product of 1 and 6 is 6.

9. The correct answer is 'A'

The prime numbers between 1 and 10 are 2, 3, 5, 7.

10. The correct answer is 'C'

Of the answer choices, 24 is the only multiple of 12.

Fractions

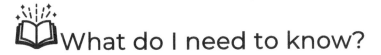

What do I need to know?

Adding and Subtracting Fractions	Make common denominators. Add or subtract the numerators and keep the denominators the same
Multiplying Fractions	Multiply the numerators and the denominators
Dividing Fractions	Turn it into a multiplication problem by flipping the second fraction and multiplying.
What about mixed numbers?	You can add or subtract mixed numbers, but for multiplication and division you need improper fractions.

 ## Example: $1\frac{1}{3} \div \frac{1}{2}$

1. Make the mixed number an improper fraction	$1\frac{1}{3} \rightarrow \frac{4}{3}$
2. Turn it into a multiplication problem by flipping the second fraction.	$\frac{4}{3} \div \frac{1}{2} \rightarrow \frac{4}{3} \times \frac{2}{1}$
3. Multiply across the top and the bottom	$\frac{4}{3} \times \frac{2}{1} = \frac{8}{3}$

1. $\frac{1}{3} + \frac{2}{5}$

   (A) $\frac{3}{15}$

   (B) $\frac{7}{15}$

   (C) $\frac{3}{8}$

   (D) $\frac{11}{15}$

2. $\frac{2}{5} \div \frac{1}{4}$

   (A) $\frac{7}{20}$

   (B) $\frac{5}{8}$

   (C) $1\frac{3}{5}$

   (D) $\frac{1}{10}$

3. $1\frac{2}{7} + 2\frac{1}{2}$

   (A) $3\frac{1}{3}$

   (B) $3\frac{3}{14}$

   (C) $3\frac{11}{14}$

   (D) $3\frac{3}{7}$

4. $\frac{3}{4} + \frac{5}{6} - \frac{1}{4}$

   (A) $\frac{1}{6}$

   (B) $\frac{3}{2}$

   (C) $\frac{5}{3}$

   (D) $\frac{4}{3}$

5. $1\frac{2}{3} \times 4\frac{1}{5}$

   (A) $4\frac{2}{15}$

   (B) 7

   (C) $\frac{21}{5}$

   (D) $7\frac{1}{5}$

6. $\frac{40\,(50+70)}{80}$

   (A) 48

   (B) 60

   (C) 480

   (D) 600

7. $\frac{5}{3} - \frac{10}{9}$

(A) $\frac{2}{3}$

(B) $\frac{5}{2}$

(C) $1\frac{2}{3}$

(D) 1

8. $\frac{1}{3} \times \frac{9}{2}$

(A) $\frac{3}{2}$

(B) $\frac{5}{2}$

(C) $\frac{2}{3}$

(D) $\frac{1}{4}$

9. $\frac{2}{5} - \frac{1}{10}$

(A) $\frac{1}{10}$

(B) $\frac{3}{10}$

(C) $\frac{2}{15}$

(D) $\frac{1}{5}$

10. $\frac{8}{5} \times \frac{5}{4}$

(A) $\frac{32}{25}$

(B) $\frac{5}{8}$

(C) 2

(D) $\frac{1}{2}$

Fractions - Answers and Explanations

1. The correct answer is 'D'

$$\frac{1}{3} + \frac{2}{5}$$

$1 \times 5 = 5$

$3 \times 5 = 15$

$$\frac{1}{3} = \frac{5}{15}$$

$2 \times 3 = 6$

$5 \times 3 = 15$

$$\frac{2}{5} = \frac{6}{15}$$

$$\frac{5}{15} + \frac{6}{15} = \frac{11}{15}$$

2. The correct answer is 'C'

$$\frac{2}{5} \div \frac{1}{4}$$

$$\frac{2}{5} \times \frac{4}{1} = \frac{8}{5} = 1\frac{3}{5}$$

3. The correct answer is 'C'

When adding and subtracting mixed numbers, you don't need to make them improper fractions. You can break it up! This is NOT the same for multiplication and division.

$$1\frac{2}{7} + 2\frac{1}{2}$$

$1 + 2 = 3$

$$\frac{4}{14} + \frac{7}{14} = \frac{11}{14} + 3 = 3\frac{11}{14}$$

4. The correct answer is 'D'

$$\frac{38}{24} - \frac{1}{4}$$

$$= \frac{38}{24} - \frac{6}{24} = \frac{32}{24} = \frac{4}{3}$$

5. The correct answer is 'B'

$$1\frac{2}{3} \times 4\frac{1}{5}$$

$$\frac{5}{3} \times \frac{21}{5} \rightarrow \frac{1}{3} \times \frac{21}{1} \rightarrow \frac{21}{3} = 7$$

6. The correct answer is 'B'

$$\frac{40\,(50+70)}{80}$$

$$40\frac{(120)}{80} \rightarrow \frac{1\,(120)}{2} \rightarrow 60$$

7. The correct answer is 'A'

$$\frac{5}{3} - \frac{10}{9} \rightarrow \frac{15}{9} - \frac{10}{9} \rightarrow \frac{5}{9}$$

8. The correct answer is 'A'

$$\frac{1}{3} \times \frac{9}{2} \rightarrow \frac{9}{6} \rightarrow \frac{3}{2}$$

9. The correct answer is 'B'

$$\frac{2}{5} - \frac{1}{10} \rightarrow \frac{4}{10} - \frac{1}{10} \rightarrow \frac{3}{10}$$

10. The correct answer is 'C'

$$\frac{8}{5} \times \frac{5}{4} \rightarrow \frac{8}{5} \times \frac{5}{4} \rightarrow \frac{8}{4} \rightarrow 2$$

Fraction Word Problems

What do I need to know?

In math, **OF** means **times**. So, if you are looking for the fraction OF something, multiply!

Example:

Don has 60 students in his grade. 2/5 of the students in Don's grade are boys. How many students in the grade are boys?

Remember *of* means ×

2/5 of the 60 students are boys SO $\frac{2}{5} \times 60$ are boys

$\frac{2}{5} \times 60 \rightarrow \frac{120}{5} = 24$

24 students are boys

Common Tricky Question Types

Sometimes you are just given a part and have to find the whole. These may be tricky but can be simple if you break it down into unit fractions (fractions with a 1 on top)!

You may get a problem like this:
Sam filled 4/5 of the pool in 60 min. How long will it take him to fill the rest of the pool?

Just, break it down!
4/5 = 60 min   SO   1/5 = 20 min
He has 1/5 left so the answer is 20 minutes.

1. Jameson ran 6 km in 3/5 of an hour. How far would he run if he ran for one hour?

   (A) 8 km

   (B) 4 km

   (C) 6 km

   (D) 10 km

2. It takes 16 minutes to fill a 4/7 of a tank. How much longer would it take to fill the whole tank?

   (A) 4

   (B) 8

   (C) 12

   (D) 16

3. 3/4 of the class wants chicken fingers for lunch. 40% of those who want chicken fingers also want fries. What fraction of the class wants chicken fingers and fries?

   (A) 1/10

   (B) 1/5

   (C) 3/10

   (D) 3/5

4. 5200 people visit a fair in a small town. Of those people 40% go for a ride on the giant wheel. What is the number of people who took a ride on the giant wheel?

   (A) 2002

   (B) 2010

   (C) 2020

   (D) 2080

5. 208 children visit a park over the course of an entire Sunday. Of them, 156 bring their pet along with them. What fraction of children who visited the park brought their pets along?

   (A) $\frac{4}{5}$

   (B) $\frac{2}{3}$

   (C) $\frac{7}{10}$

   (D) $\frac{3}{4}$

6. Carlin and Anya have 5 buckets of water balloons. Carlin uses 1/2 of each bucket. Anya uses 2/5 of each bucket. How many buckets of water balloons are left?

   (A) 1/5

   (B) 1/2

   (C) 2/3

   (D) 1

7. A man decides to take a walk for 2 km. He walks for $\frac{1}{2}$ the distance and rests. Then he takes a lift on his friend's bike for $\frac{2}{3}$ of the remaining distance and walks for the rest. How many kilometers did he travel on foot?

(A) $\frac{1}{2}$ km

(B) $1\frac{1}{3}$ km

(C) 1 km

(D) $1\frac{2}{3}$ km

8. Heidi has 40 fish. She sells $\frac{2}{5}$ of fish at the school fair. $\frac{5}{8}$ of the remaining fish are gold. The rest are blue. How many blue fish does Heidi have left?

(A) 12

(B) 9

(C) 15

(D) 10

9. An ice-cream truck reports having sold 21 chocolate flavored, 14 vanilla flavored and 7 strawberry flavored ice-creams in one day. What fraction of the total sales were strawberry or vanilla?

(A) $\frac{1}{2}$

(B) $\frac{3}{4}$

(C) $\frac{1}{4}$

(D) $\frac{3}{5}$

10. A group of bird watchers spots 4 blue, 6 red and 7 black birds on Sunday morning. On Monday, they come back to spot 2 blue, 4 red and 7 black birds. What fraction of the birds spotted both Sunday and Monday were blue?

(A) $\frac{1}{5}$

(B) $\frac{2}{13}$

(C) $\frac{4}{17}$

(D) $\frac{2}{30}$

1. **The correct answer is 'D'**

Jameson ran 6 km in 3/5 of an hour. How far would he run if he ran for one hour?

6 km in 3/5 of an hour --> Divide by 3

2 km in 1/5 of an hour --> x 5

10 km in 5/5 of an hour or 1 hour

10 km

2. **The correct answer is 'C'**

It takes 16 minutes to fill a 4/7 of a tank. How much longer would it take to fill the whole tank?

4/7 = 16 minutes

1/7 = 4 minutes

3/7 = 12 minutes

3. **The correct answer is 'C'**

40% OF 3/4

4/10 x 3/4

2/5 x 3/4

6/20 --> 3/10

4. **The correct answer is 'D'**

40% of 5200 people took a ride on the giant wheel

$\frac{40}{100} \times 5200 \rightarrow \frac{40}{100} \times 5200 \rightarrow 40 \times 52 =$

2080

5. **The correct answer is 'D'**

156 out of 208 children brought their pets to the park. So, the required fraction is

$\frac{156}{208} = \frac{78}{104} = \frac{39}{52} = \frac{3}{4}$.

6. **The correct answer is 'B'**

1/2 x 5 = 5/2 --> 2 1/2. Carlin uses 2 1/2

2/5 x 5 = 2--> Anya uses 2 buckets

5 - 4 1/2 = 1/2

1/2 Bucket is left.

7. **The correct answer is 'B'.**

The man walks $\frac{1}{2} \times 2$ km=1km before resting. The remaining distance is 1km. He travels $\frac{2}{3}$ km on his friend's bike. The remaining distance of $\frac{1}{3}$ km he walks. So total distance covered by him on foot is $1 + \frac{1}{3} = 1\frac{1}{3}$ km.

8. **The correct answer is 'B'**

$\frac{2}{5} \times 40 = 16$ fish were sold. The remaining number of fish is 24.

$\frac{5}{8}$ of the remaining fish are gold.

$\frac{5}{8} \times 24 = 15$

So, 9 fish are blue.

9. **The correct answer is 'A'**

The total number of vanilla and strawberry flavored ice-creams is $14 + 7 = 21$.

The total number of ice-creams sold is $21 + 14 + 7 = 21 + 21 = 42$.

So, the required fraction is $\frac{21}{42} = \frac{1}{2}$.

10. **The correct answer is 'A'**

They spotted 4 blue birds on Sunday and 2 on Monday. $4+2 = 6$

They spotted 30 birds total $(4 + 6 + 7 + 2 + 4 + 7 = 30)$

$$\frac{6 \; blue \; birds}{30 \; total \; birds} \dashrightarrow \frac{6}{30} = \frac{1}{5}$$

Decimals

What do I need to know?

Adding and Subtracting Decimals	Line up the decimals and add or subtract as you normally would	4.12 +3.2 7.32
Multiplying Decimals	Multiply as if there are no decimals. After, count the number of digits after both numbers in the problem. Put the decimal the same number of digits after the decimal in the answer.	4.12 x 3.2 412 x 32 = 13184 In the initial problem, there are 3 digits total behind the decimals. The solution is 13.184
Dividing Decimals	Take the decimal out of the divisor by multiplying both numbers by 10. Then, divide normally.	6.72 ÷ 2.1 Multiply both by 10 to get rid of the decimal in the divisor 67.2 ÷ 21 Then, divide normally and keep the decimal where it was in the dividend. $\underline{3.2}$ 21⟌67.2
Fractions → Decimals	You can turn any fraction into a division problem to find its value as a decimal.	$\frac{2}{5}$→ 2 ÷ 5 $\underline{.4}$ 5⟌2.0

What should I memorize?

It is helpful to memorize a few fraction→ decimal conversions.

$\frac{1}{2}$ = 0.5 $\frac{1}{3}$ = 0.33... $\frac{1}{4}$= 0.25 $\frac{1}{5}$ = 0.2 $\frac{2}{3}$ = 0.66... $\frac{3}{4}$ = 0.75 $\frac{2}{5}$ = 0.4

1. 394.32 is the same as

(A) $394 + \frac{3}{1} + \frac{2}{10}$

(B) $394 + \frac{3}{10} + \frac{2}{100}$

(C) $394 + \frac{3}{100} + \frac{2}{1000}$

(D) $394 + \frac{3}{10} + \frac{2}{1000}$

2. What is the value of the expression:

3.1 + 2.45 + 0.05 + 6.1?

(A) 3.42

(B) 12.15

(C) 11.7

(D) 11.4

3. What is the value of the expression:

4.42 x 2.1?

(A) 0.9282

(B) 9.282

(C) 92.82

(D) 928.2

4. Evaluate the following expression: 28 ÷ 2.5

(A) 1.12

(B) 11.2

(C) 1.22

(D) 12.2

5. What fraction is equal to 0.16?

(A) $\frac{4}{25}$

(B) $\frac{1}{5}$

(C) $\frac{2}{3}$

(D) $\frac{1}{16}$

6. Evaluate the following expression: $\frac{1}{2}$ + $0.4 + \frac{3}{4}$ + 0.62

(A) 1.77

(B) 2.27

(C) 7.85

(D) 9.02

7. Evaluate (2 × 5.4) + 1.4

(A) 11.2

(B) 11.8

(C) 12.2

(D) 12.8

8. Which value lies between $\frac{1}{3}$ and $\frac{1}{2}$?

(A) 0.25

(B) 0.45

(C) 0.68

(D) 0.15

9. You have 2 chocolates. Your friend gives you 2.5 times as many chocolates How many chocolates do you have now?

(A) 4.5

(B) 3

(C) 7

(D) 8

10. What is the value of the expression 2.6 × 3.2?

(A) 0.832

(B) 8.23

(C) 8.32

(D) 832

Decimals - Answers and Explanation

1. The correct answer is 'B

$$394 = 394$$

$$0.3 = \frac{3}{10}$$

$$0.02 = \frac{2}{100}$$

B is correct- $394 + \frac{3}{10} + \frac{2}{100}$

2. The correct answer is 'C'

Make sure you line up the decimals!

```
   3.1
   2.45
   0.05
 + 6.1
 11 .70
```

3. The correct answer is 'B'

The decimal is 2 places over in 4.42 and 1 place over in 2.1, so you will move it 3 places over when you get your answer. You could also do this one by estimating since the answer choices are far apart. 4 * 2= 8, so 9 would be closest. 9.282 is correct.

4. The correct answer is 'B'

Move the decimal over one place in the numerator and the denominator so you have 280/25. This is an equivalent expression and you do not need to adjust your answer at all afterward.

280/25 = 11.2

5. The correct answer is 'A'

$$0.16 = \frac{16}{100} = \frac{4}{25}$$

6. The correct answer is 'B'

Remember the conversions! $\frac{1}{2} = 0.5$ and $\frac{3}{4} = 0.75$

Then, line up the decimals

```
   0.5
   0.4
   0.75
 + 0.62
   2.27
```

7. The correct answer is 'C'

$$(2 \times 5.4) + 1.4$$

$$(2 \times 5.4) = 10.8$$

$$10.8 + 1.4 = 12.2$$

8. The correct answer is 'B'.

$$\frac{1}{3} = 0 \cdot 333 \ldots \text{ and } \frac{1}{2} = 0 \cdot 5$$

The only value in the options that lies between these numbers is 0.45.

9. The correct answer is 'C'.

2.5 × 2 = 5 chocolates were given by the friend. Therefore, the total number of chocolates now is

2 + 5 = 7.

10. The correct answer is 'C'

$$2.6 \times 3.2$$

$$26 \times 32 = 832$$

In the original problem, the decimal is two places over total. So, it needs to be two places over in the solution. 832 → 8.32

Percents

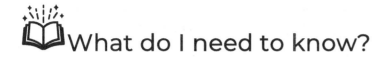

What do I need to know?

Converting Fractions to Percents	Multiply by 100	$\frac{1}{5} \times \frac{100}{1} = 20\%$
Converting Decimals to Percents	Multiply by 100	$0.42 \times 100 = 42\%$
Finding the Percent of a Number	Multiply the number by the percentage in decimal or fraction form.	What is 20% of 40? $20\% = \frac{1}{5}$ $\frac{1}{5} \times \frac{40}{1} = 8$

Any tricks?

A fast way to find the percent of a number is to break it up into smaller percentages. For example, if 100% is 40, 10% is 4. With this, we can find that 20% is 8 or that 5% is 2.

Example: What is 15% of 280?

10% = 28

5% = 14

So, 15% = 28 + 14 = 42

Common Tricky Question Type

The original price of an item was $100

Column A	Column B
The amount saved after a 20% discount	The amount saved after two separate 10% discounts

(A) Column A is greater

(B) Column B is greater

(C) Column A and Column B are equal

(D) The relationship cannot be determined with the information given

At first, it may seem like the amount saved would be equal because 10% + 10% = 20%. BUT when you take two discounts separately, you always end up with a less of a discount than when you take the full chunk at once.

Let's see how that works:

Column A

20% of $100 = $20

Column B

10% of $100 = $10

New Price = $90

10% of $90 = $9

Total saved = $10 + $9 = $19

So, when you take the full discount all at once, you save MORE than when you take the same percent in two separate discounts.

1. Write $\frac{3}{5}$ as a percent:

   (A) 3%

   (B) 30%

   (C) 6%

   (D) 60%

2. Write $\frac{5}{18}$ as a percent. Round to the nearest hundredth.

   (A) 2.77%

   (B) 27.77%

   (C) 2.47%

   (D) 24.77%

3. What is 36% of 150?

   (A) 30

   (B) 48

   (C) 54

   (D) 60

4. What is 15% of 140?

   (A) 14

   (B) 18

   (C) 21

   (D) 24

5. Kara wrote 18 postcards. She then wrote 150% more the next day. How many postcards did she write in all?

   (A) 27

   (B) 26

   (C) 45

   (D) 54

6. The original price of an item was $100

Column A	Column B
The amount saved after a 40% discount	The amount saved after two separate 20% discounts

   (A) Column A is greater

   (B) Column B is greater

   (C) Column A and Column B are equal

   (D) The relationship cannot be determined with the information given

7. Which of the following values is greater?

The original price of a car was $10,000

Column A	**Column B**
The amount saved after two separate 13% discounts	The amount saved after a 26% discount

(A) Column A is greater

(B) Column B is greater

(C) Column A and Column B are equal

(D) The relationship cannot be determined with the information given

8. Jared made 64 brownies for a bake sale one day. The next day he made 150% more. How many cookies did he make in total?

(A) 64

(B) 96

(C) 128

(D) 160

9. Kara gave her friend 35% of her chewing gum. Kara initially had 120 pieces of gum. How many pieces did she give her friend?

(A) 24

(B) 36

(C) 42

(D) 48

10. A new hardcover book costs $30. On Tuesdays, there is a 20% discount on all hardcover books. How much does the book cost on Tuesdays

(A) $6

(B) $22

(C) $24

(D) $25

1. **The correct answer is 'D'**

   $\frac{3}{5} \times \frac{100}{1} = \frac{300}{5} = 60\%$

2. **The correct answer is 'B'**

   $\frac{5}{18} \times 100 = \frac{500}{18} \rightarrow 500 \div 18 = 27.77\%$

3. **The correct answer is 'C'**

   $\frac{150}{1} \times \frac{36}{100} = \frac{3}{1} \times \frac{18}{1} = 54$

4. **The correct answer is 'C'**

   15% of 140

   10% = 14

   5% = 7

   14 + 7 = 21

5. **The correct answer is 'C'**

   18 + 150% of 18

   100% of 18 = 18

   50% of 18 = 9

   18 + 18 + 9 = 45

6. **The correct answer is 'A'**

   When the total of the percent discounts seems to be equal, the single discount will always be greater. The second discount in Column B is taking 20% off of a lesser amount.

7. **The correct answer is 'B'**

   When the total of the percent discounts seem to be equal, the single discount will always be greater. The second discount in Column A is taking 13% off of a lesser amount.

8. **The correct answer is 'D'**

   100%= 64

   50% = 32

   150%= 96

   96 + 64 = 160

9. **The correct answer is 'C'**

   120

   10% = 12 --> 30% = 12 x 3 = 36

   5% = 6

   35% = 36 + 6 = 42

10. **The correct answer is 'C'**

    100% = 30

    10% = 3

    20% = 6

    30-6 = 24 --> $24

Negative Numbers

What do I need to know?

Adding Negative Numbers	A negative number goes down on the number line, so if you add a negative number, you are subtracting	$5 + -4$ $5 - 4$ 1 $-5 + -4$ $-5 - 4$ -9
Subtracting Negative Numbers	If you subtract a negative, it becomes a positive. HINT: If you see - - turn it into +	$5 - -4$ $5 + 4$ 9
Multiplying and Dividing Negative Numbers	When multiplying and dividing, pairs of negatives cancel each other out. $- \times + = -$ $- \times - = +$	$-4 \times 3 = -12$ $-4 \times -3 = 12$

Example:

$$-4(-5) + -3 + 4$$

Remember to follow PEMDAS

$$-4(-5) + -3 + 4$$
$$20 + -3 + 4$$
$$20 - 3 + 4$$
$$17 + 4$$
$$21$$

1. $-3-2$

   (A) -5

   (B) -2

   (C) -1

   (D) 5

2. $-3+7-2$

   (A) -12

   (B) -8

   (C) -2

   (D) 2

3. $-3(-6)$

   (A) -18

   (B) -9

   (C) 9

   (D) 18

4. $2(-4)-5$

   (A) -3

   (B) 3

   (C) -13

   (D) 13

5. $(-8) \times (-3)$

   (A) -12

   (B) -24

   (C) 12

   (D) 24

6. $-3(-4)+5(-3)$

   (A) -3

   (B) 3

   (C) -27

   (D) 27

7. $-4+1-3$

   (A) -6

   (B) -4

   (C) -2

   (D) 3

8. $4-9+25$

   (A) 16

   (B) 20

   (C) 24

   (D) 18

9. $-\frac{3}{2} \times 2$

   (A) -3

   (B) -2

   (C) 2

   (D) 3

10. $-4+3-2$

   (A) -2

   (B) -3

   (C) 2

   (D) 3

1. **The correct answer is 'A'**

   Start at - 3 and go down 2 more, so you

   get to – 5

2. **The correct answer is 'D'**

   - 3 + 7 - 2

   - 3 + 7 = 4

   4 - 2 = 2

   2

3. **The correct answer is 'D'**

   3 x 6 = 18

   AND

   a negative x a negative = a positive

   So, -3(-6)= 18

4. **The correct answer is 'C'**

   2 (- 4) = - 8

   - 8 - 5 = - 13

5. **The correct answer is 'D'**

   -8×-3

   8×3

   24

6. **The correct answer is 'A'**

   - 3(- 4) + 5(- 3)

   12 - 15

   -3

7. **The correct answer is 'A'**

   $-4 + 1 - 3$

   $-3 - 3$

   -6

8. **The correct answer is 'B'**

   $4 - 9 + 25$

   $-5 + 25$

   20

9. **The correct answer is 'A'**

   $-\frac{3}{2} \times 2 = -\frac{3}{2} \times \frac{2}{1} = -\frac{6}{2} = -3$

10. **The correct answer is 'B'**

   $-4 + 3 - 2$

   $= -1 - 2$

   $= -3$

Exponents and Roots

 ## What do I need to know?

Exponents	An exponent refers to the number of times a number is multiplied by itself	$4^3 = 4 \times 4 \times 4$
Negatives and Exponents	A negative is only used for with the exponent if it is in parenthesis. If not, add it on at the end. Remember, pairs of negatives cancel each other out in multiplication.	$-4^2 = -16$ $(-4)^2 = 16$
Square Roots	The square root of a number is the value that when multiplied by itself will give you that number.	$\sqrt{16} = 4$ because $4 \times 4 = 16$
Square Roots and Arithmetic	If two numbers are being multiplied under a square root sign, you can break it up. If they are being added or subtracted, you cannot do this.	$\sqrt{4 \times 9} = \sqrt{4} \times \sqrt{9}$ BUT $\sqrt{4 + 9}$ IS NOT $\sqrt{4} + \sqrt{9}$

Example: $(-3)^4$

$$(-3)^4$$

$$-3 \times -3 \times -3 \times -3$$

$$3 \times 3 \times 3 \times 3$$

$$81$$

1. 5^3

    (A) 15

    (B) 25

    (C) 50

    (D) 125

2. Which of the following is greater?

Column A	**Column B**
-3^2	9

    (A) Column A is greater

    (B) Column B is greater

    (C) Column A and B are equal

    (D) The answer cannot be determined with the information provided

3. $(-2)^4$

    (A) -16

    (B) 16

    (C) -8

    (D) 8

4. $\sqrt{4 + 12}$

    (A) 4

    (B) 5

    (C) 8

    (D) 16

5. $\sqrt{9 \times 25}$

    (A) 10

    (B) 15

    (C) 20

    (D) 25

6. Which of the following values is greater?

Column A	**Column B**
$\sqrt{16 \times 25}$	$\sqrt{16} \times \sqrt{25}$

    (A) Column A is greater

    (B) Column B is greater

    (C) Column A and Column B are equal

    (D) The relationship cannot be determined with the information given

7. Which of the following values is greater?

Column A	**Column B**
$\sqrt{25 + 49}$	$\sqrt{25} + \sqrt{49}$

    (A) Column A is greater

    (B) Column B is greater

    (C) Column A and Column B are equal

    (D) The relationship cannot be determined with the information given

8. Which of the following values is greater?

Column A	Column B
-5^4	$(-5)^4$

   (A) Column A is greater

   (B) Column B is greater

   (C) Column A and Column B are equal

   (D) The relationship cannot be determined with the information given

9. Which of the following values is greater?

Column A	Column B
-4^4	64

   (A) Column A is greater

   (B) Column B is greater

   (C) Column A and Column B are equal

   (D) The relationship cannot be determined with the information given

10. Which of the following values greater?

Column A	Column B
$\sqrt{16 \times 25}$	$(-4)^3$

   (A) Column A is greater

   (B) Column B is greater

   (C) Column A and Column B are equal

   (D) The relationship cannot be determined with the information given

1. The correct answer is 'D'

  5 x 5 x 5 = 125

2. The correct answer is 'B'

  Because the negative is not in

  parenthesis, it is added on at the end.

  - (3 x 3) = - 9

  Column B is greater

3. The correct answer is 'B'

  Because the negative is inside the

  parenthesis, it is included when being

  multiplied. Because it is multiplied an

  EVEN number of times, the negatives

  cancel each other out so the answer is

  positive.

$$(-2)^4$$

$$(- 2) (- 2) (- 2) (- 2)$$

$$4 (- 2) (- 2)$$

$$-8 (- 2)$$

16

4. The correct answer is 'A'

$$\sqrt{4 + 12} = \sqrt{16} = 4$$

  4 x 4 = 16

5. The correct answer is 'B'

$$\sqrt{9 \times 25} = \sqrt{9} \times \sqrt{25} = 3 \times 5 = 15$$

6. The correct answer is 'C'

  When multiplying inside a radical, you

  can break up the radical. The answer will

  be the same.

7. The correct answer is 'B'

  These are NOT the same. With addition,

  they have to be solved as is since they

  produce different answers.

  Column A: The square root of 74 ~8.9

  Column B: 5 + 7 = 12

8. The correct answer is 'B'

  When the negative is NOT in parentheses,

  it is added on at the end so it stays

  negative. When it is inside parentheses, it

  is multiplied so the answer will become

  positive since it is multiplied an even

  number of times.

9. The correct answer is 'B'

  When the negative is NOT in parentheses,

  it is added on at the end so it stays

  negative. Column A: Negative

  Column B: Positive

10. The correct answer is 'A'

  Column A: Positive

  Column B: Negative $(-4 \times -4 \times -4 =$

$$-64$$

Arithmetic Review

1. What is 35% of 220?

   (A) 67

   (B) 77

   (C) 80

   (D) 87

2. There are six buckets filled with sand. Marcus used $\frac{1}{4}$ of each bucket of sand. Jasmine used $\frac{2}{3}$ of each bucket. How many buckets remain?

   (A) $\frac{1}{4}$

   (B) $\frac{1}{3}$

   (C) $\frac{1}{2}$

   (D) $\frac{2}{3}$

3. What is the greatest common factor of 24 and 30?

   (A) 3

   (B) 6

   (C) 120

   (D) 720

4. Yesterday, Marlee baked 120 cookies. She then baked 125% more today. How many cookies did she bake in all?

   (A) 120

   (B) 150

   (C) 240

   (D) 270

5. 4.53 is the same as...

   (A) $4 + \frac{5}{100} + \frac{3}{1000}$

   (B) $4 + \frac{5}{10} + \frac{3}{100}$

   (C) $4 + \frac{5}{1} + \frac{3}{10}$

   (D) $4 + \frac{5}{10} + \frac{3}{1000}$

6. Which of the following is greater?

Column A	Column B
$(-3)^6$	-3^6

   (A) Column A is greater

   (B) Column B is greater

   (C) Column A and Column B are equal

   (D) The answer cannot be determined with the information provided

7. $(-2 + 4) + 3^2 - 4 \times 2$

   (A) 1

   (B) 3

   (C) 6

   (D) 14

8. Which of the following numbers is prime?

   (A) 363

   (B) 585

   (C) 468

   (D) 479

9. What is the value of the expression

2.4 + 3.12 + 0.02 + 4.02?

(A) 9.56

(B) 9.64

(C) 6.8

(D) 6.86

10. $\sqrt{16 \times 36}$

(A) 23

(B) 24

(C) $\sqrt{586}$

(D) $\sqrt{52}$

11. What is the value of the expression: 3.4 ×

2.43?

(A) 0.8262

(B) 8.262

(C) 82.62

(D) 826.2

12. 60% of the people in the class were

wearing jeans. $\frac{2}{3}$ of those students

wearing jeans were also wearing

sneakers. What fraction of the class was

wearing jeans and sneakers?

(A) $\frac{2}{5}$

(B) $\frac{1}{3}$

(C) $\frac{7}{15}$

(D) $\frac{3}{5}$

13. −5 (−2) + 10 − 5 − 3 × 3

(A) -14

(B) 4

(C) 6

(D) 36

14. $3\frac{2}{3} \div 1\frac{5}{6}$

(A) 1

(B) 2

(C) 3

(D) 6

15. $\frac{1}{4} + 0.43 + \frac{3}{5} + 1.24$

(A) 2.12

(B) 2.32

(C) 2.52

(D) 2.72

Arithmetic Review - Answers and Explanations

1. The correct answer is 'B'

10% of 220 = 22

5% = 11 (Half of 10%)

30% = 66 (10% x 3 OR 22 x 3)

35% = 77 (30% + 5%)

2. The correct answer is 'C'

If Marcus used $\frac{1}{4}$ of each, he used $6 \times \frac{1}{4}$, SO,

$\frac{6}{4}$ or 1.5.

If Jasmine used $\frac{2}{3}$ of each, she used $6 \times \frac{2}{3}$,

SO, $\frac{12}{3}$ or 4.

They used 1.5 + 4 or 5.5 buckets together,

so $\frac{1}{2}$ bucket remains.

3. The correct answer is 'B'

High factors of 24: 12, 8, 6

High factors of 30: 10, 6, 5

6 is the greatest common factor

4. The correct answer is 'D'

50% of 120 = 60 SO 25% = 30

125% = 120 + 30 = 150

120(Yesterday) + 150(Today) = 270

5. The correct answer is 'B'

4.53

4 = 4

$\frac{5}{10} = 0.5$

$\frac{3}{100} = 0.03$

6. The correct answer is 'A'

Column A is greater. Because the negative is in parenthesis, it is included in the exponent function. The number is multiplied an even number of times, so it will end up being positive. For Column B, the negative is added on after performing the exponent function, so the answer will be negative.

7. The correct answer is 'B'

$(-2 + 4) + 3^2 - 4 \times 2$

$2 + 3^2 - 4 \times 2$

$2 + 9 - 4 \times 2$

$2 + 9 - 8$

$11 - 8$

3

8. The correct answer is 'D'

363: 3 + 6 + 3 = 12 SO, divisible by 3

585: Ends in a 5, SO divisible by 5

468: Ends in an even number, SO divisible by 2

479 is prime

9. The correct answer is 'A'

$$4.02$$
$$3.12$$
$$2.4$$
$$\underline{+\ 0.02}$$
$$9.56$$

10. The correct answer is 'B'

$$\sqrt{16 \times 36} = \sqrt{16} \times \sqrt{36} = 4 \times 6 = 24$$

11. The correct answer is 'B'

The decimal is 1 place over in 3.4 and 2 places over in 2.43, so you will move it 3 places over when you get your answer. You could also do this one by estimating since the answer choices are far apart. 3 x 2= 6, so 8 would be closest. **8.262 is correct.**

12. The correct answer is 'A'

Remember, in math, OF = ×

We are looking for $\frac{2}{3}$ OF 60% (60% = $\frac{6}{10}$ or $\frac{3}{5}$)

$$\frac{2}{3} \times \frac{3}{5} = \frac{6}{16} \text{ or } \frac{2}{5}$$

13. The correct answer is 'C'

$$-5\ (-2) + 10 - 5 - 3 \times 3$$
$$10 + 10 - 5 - 9$$
$$20 - 5 - 9$$
$$15 - 9$$
$$6$$

14. The correct answer is 'B'

$$3\frac{2}{3} \div 1\frac{5}{6}$$
$$3 = \frac{9}{3} + \frac{2}{3} = \frac{11}{3}$$
$$1 = \frac{6}{6} + \frac{5}{6} = \frac{11}{6}$$
$$\frac{11}{3} \times \frac{6}{11} = \frac{6}{3} = \mathbf{2}$$

15. The correct answer is 'C'

$$\frac{1}{4} + 0.43 + \frac{3}{5} + 1.24$$

Memorizing your basic fraction--> decimal conversions will help here!

$$\frac{1}{4} = 0.25$$
$$\frac{1}{5} = 0.2 \text{ SO } \frac{3}{5} = 0.6$$
$$0.25 + 0.43 + 0.6 + 1.24$$
$$1.24$$
$$0.6$$
$$0.43$$
$$\underline{+\ 0.25}$$
$$2.52$$

Algebra

Substitution and Strange Symbols

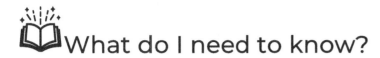

What do I need to know?

Basic Substitution	Take the number given for the variable and insert it into the expression in the place of the variable	If x = 3, what is 4x? 4x → 4(3) 12
Substitution with Strange Symbols	If you see an odd symbol next to a variable, this means that you should substitute the number given next to the symbol for the variable in the expression	For any number @k, @k = k+3 What is @4? All this means is to substitute 4 for k. k+ 3 → 4 + 3 7

Common Tricky Question Types

Strange symbols are a common type of tricky question on the ISEE. They look confusing, but all you need to do is substitute the variable after the symbol the number given.

Example:

For any number &r, &r = 4r - 2

What is &3?

All this means is to substitute 3 for r.

&3 = 4(3) − 2

12 − 2 = **10**

1. If x = 4, what is -3x + 8?

   (A) -20

   (B) -4

   (C) 4

   (D) 20

2. If a = 4 and b = 3, what is 4a - 3b + 2?

   (A) 2

   (B) 5

   (C) 9

   (D) 11

3. For any number &f, &f = 5f + 3

   What is the value of &6?

   (A) 30

   (B) 33

   (C) 59

   (D) 60

4. For any number p*g, p*g= 4p - 2g - 5

   What is the value of 5*4?

   (A) 1

   (B) 7

   (C) 10

   (D) 23

5. 3$ = 4* and 2* = 3@

   If $ = 8, what is the value of @?

   (A) 3

   (B) 4

   (C) 5

   (D) 6

6. For any number a^, a^= 2a - 4

   What is the value of 3^?

   (A) 1

   (B) 2

   (C) 4

   (D) 6

7. For any number g#, g#= 10 - 4g

   What is the value of 4#?

   (A) -10

   (B) -6

   (C) 0

   (D) 4

8. For any number a*b, a*b= 5a - 3b - 5

   What is the value of 6*5?

   (A) 10

   (B) 15

   (C) 20

   (D) 30

9. For any number @f, @f= 12 + 2f

   What is the value of @6?

   (A) 6

   (B) 12

   (C) 24

   (D) 38

10. 3# = 4^ and 2^ = 6&. If # = 8, what is the value of &?

   (A) 1

   (B) 2

   (C) 4

   (D) 6

1. The correct answer is 'B'

-3(4) + 8

-12 + 8

-4

2. The correct answer is 'C'

a = 4 and b = 3

4a - 3b + 2

4(4) - 3(3) + 2

16 - 9 +2

9

3. The correct answer is 'B'

For any number &f, &f = 5f + 3

What is the value of &6?

Substitute when f = 6

5(6) + 3

30 + 3

33

4. The correct answer is 'B'

For any number p*g, p*g= 4p - 2g - 5

What is the value of 5*4?

Substitute! p = 5, g = 4

4(5) - 2(4) - 5

20 - 8 - 5

7

5. The correct answer is 'B'

 3$ = 4* and 2* = 3@

If $ = 8, what is the value of @?

3(8) = 4*, 4* = 24 SO 2* = 12

3@=12 SO @=4

6. The correct answer is 'B'

a = 3

2(3) - 4

6 - 4

2

7. The correct answer is 'B'

g = 4

10 - 4 (4)

10 - 16

- 6

8. The correct answer is 'A'

a= 6

b = 5

5(6) - 3(5) - 5

30 -15 -5

10

9. The correct answer is 'C'

f = 6

12 + 2(6)

12 + 12

24

10. The correct answer is 'B'

= 8 SO 3# = 3(8)= 24

24 = 4^ SO 2^ = 12

12 = 6& SO & = **2**

Combining Like Terms

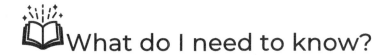

What do I need to know?

Like terms are parts of an expression with the same variable raised to the same power. In algebra, you can ONLY combine like terms. So, $2x^2 + x^2 = 3x^2$ because they both have the same variable raised to the same power.

$$5x^2 + 3x - x^2 + 2x - 4 + 5$$

In the expression above, all terms with x^2 are **like terms** and can be combined.
$$5x^2 - x^2 = \mathbf{4x^2}$$

In the expression above, all terms with x are like terms and can be combined.
$$3x + 2x = \mathbf{5x}$$

In the expression above, all terms with **no variables** are like terms and can be combined.
$$-4 + 5 = \mathbf{1}$$

The result is $\mathbf{4x^2 + 5x + 1}$

Example:

$4x^2 - 3x + 3x^2 - 4$

The only like terms are $4x^2$ and $3x^2$

$4x^2 + 3x^2 = 7x^2$

The result is

$7x^2 - 3x - 4$

1. $4x^2 - 2x + 3x^2 - x$

   (A) $4x^3$
   (B) $7x^2 - x$
   (C) $2x^2 - 2x$
   (D) $7x^2 - 3x$

2. $3x^2 - 3x - 5x^2 - 3$

   (A) $-2x^2 - 3x - 3$
   (B) $2x^2 - 3x - 3$
   (C) $6x^2 - 5x - 3$
   (D) $-2x^2 + 3x - 3$

3. $5x + 3x - 7x + x^2$

   (A) $2x^2$
   (B) $x - x^2$
   (C) $x^2 + x$
   (D) $-7x + x^2$

4. $4a - 3b - 2a + 6b$

   (A) $b + 3b$
   (B) $2a + 3b$
   (C) $2b + 3a$
   (D) $2a + b$

5. $3a^2 - 6a - 4a^2$

   (A) $-a(a + 6)$
   (B) $a(a + 6)$
   (C) $a(a - 6)$
   (D) $a(-a + 6)$

6. $-2x^2 + 4x + 3y - 2x + 5y$

   (A) $-2x^2 + 2x + 8y$
   (B) $-2x^2 + 4x + 8y$
   (C) $2x^2 - 2x + 8y$
   (D) $-2x^2 + 5x + 5y$

7. $7x - 9y + 3 - 3x - 5y + 8$

   (A) $4x - 14y + 11$
   (B) $2x - 4y + 10$
   (C) $3x + 5y + 13$
   (D) $4x + 7y - 1$

8. $3a + 5b - 4a + c + b$

   (A) $2a - b$
   (B) $-a + b + c$
   (C) $-a + 6b + c$
   (D) $7a + 6b$

9. $8m + 9n + p - 10m + 2p$

(A) $3n + 2p + m$

(B) $4n + 5p - 3m$

(C) $-2m + 9n + 3p$

(D) $18m + 8n + 3p$

10. $9m - 6n - 3m$

(A) $6(m - n)$

(B) $3m - 6n$

(C) $9m - 8n$

(D) $7m - 6n$

1. The correct answer is 'D'

$4x^2 + 3x^2 = 7x^2$

-2x − x = -3x

$7x^2 − 3x$

2. The correct answer is 'A'

$−2x^2 − 3x − 3$

Because $3x^2 − 5x^2 = −2x^2$

3. The correct answer is 'C'

$x^2 + x$

Because

$5x + 3x − 7x \rightarrow 8x − 7x = x$

4. The correct answer is 'B'

$2a + 3b$

Because

$4a − 2a = 2a$

$−3b + 6b = 3b$

5. The correct answer is 'A'

$3a^2 − 6a − 4a^2$

$=3a^2 − 4a^2 − 6a$

$= −a^2 − 6a$

=-a(a+6)

6. The correct answer is 'A'

$−2x^2 + 2x + 8y$

Because

$4x − 2x = 2x$

$3y + 5y = 8y$

7. The correct answer is 'A'

$7x − 3x = 4x$

$−9y − 5y = −14y$

$3 + 8 = 11$

8. The correct answer is 'C'

$3a − 4a = −a$

$5b + b = 6b$

So, the answer is $−a + 6b + c$

9. The correct answer is 'C'

$8m − 10m = −2m$

$p + 2p = 3p$

So, the answer is $−2m + 9n + 3p$

10. The correct answer is 'A'

$= 9m − 6n − 3m$

$= 9m − 3m − 6n$

$= 6m − 6n$

$= 6(m − n)$

Algebraic Equations

 What do I need to know?

When solving an algebraic equation, your goal is to **get the variable alone**. You can move the other numbers away from the variable by **performing reverse operations on both sides of the equal sign**.

For example, take x + 3 = 9. To get x alone, you need to get rid of +3. The reverse operation of + 3 is – 3. So, subtract 3 on both sides:

$x + 3 = 9$

$ - 3 \quad - 3$

$x = 6$

You can do the same with multiplication and division:

$4x = 20$

$\div 4 \quad \div 4$

$x = 5$

 Example: $3x - 2 = 7$

$$3x - 2 = 7$$
$$+2 \quad +2$$

$$3x = 9$$
$$\div 3 \quad \div 3$$

$$x = 3$$

1. Solve for x

   $3x + 8 = 7x$

   (A) 1

   (B) 2

   (C) $\frac{1}{2}$

   (D) 4

2. Solve for x

   $4x + 2 = 18$

   (A) 2

   (B) 4

   (C) 6

   (D) 8

3. Solve for x

   $x + 2 = 3x - 4$

   (A) -3

   (B) -2

   (C) 2

   (D) 3

4. Solve for x

   $3x - 4x + 12 = 2x - 9$

   (A) 5

   (B) 6

   (C) 7

   (D) 8

5. Solve for b:

   $10b + 1 = 13 - 2b$

   (A) 1

   (B) 2

   (C) 3

   (D) 0

6. Solve for x

   $\frac{x}{5} = \frac{56}{8}$

   (A) 7

   (B) 25

   (C) 35

   (D) 42

7. Solve for x: $3x + 2 = -7$

   (A) -4

   (B) -3

   (C) 3

   (D) 4

8. Solve for a:

   $3a - 4 = 4 - a$

   (A) 4

   (B) 3

   (C) 2

   (D) 1

9. Solve for x: $2x + 2 = 12$

   (A) 5

   (B) 7

   (C) 6

   (D) 4

10. Solve for x: $\frac{1}{x} + 1 = \frac{3}{2}$

    (A) 1

    (B) 3

    (C) 4

    (D) 2

1. The correct answer is 'B'

$$3x + 8 = 7x$$
$$- 3x \qquad - 3x$$
$$8 = 4x$$
$$2 = x$$

2. The correct answer is 'B'

$$4x + 2 = 18$$
$$-2 \qquad - 2$$
$$4x = 16$$
$$x = 4$$

3. The correct answer is 'D'

$$x + 2 = 3x - 4$$
$$- 2 \qquad - 2$$
$$x = 3x - 6$$
$$-3x \qquad - 3x$$
$$-2x = - 6$$
$$x = 3$$

4. The correct answer is 'C'

$$3x - 4x + 12 = 2x - 9$$
$$-x + 12 = 2x - 9$$
$$+ x \qquad + x$$
$$12 = 3x - 9$$
$$+9 \qquad + 9$$
$$21 = 3x$$
$$7 = x$$

5. The correct answer is 'A'

$$10b + 2b = 13 - 1$$
$$12b = 12$$
$$b = 1$$

6. The correct answer is 'C'

$\frac{56}{8}$ simplifies to 7

$$\frac{x}{5} = 7$$
$$x = 35$$

7. The correct answer is 'B'

$$3x + 2 = -7$$
$$-2 \quad - 2$$
$$3x = -9$$
$$\div 3 \quad \div 3$$
$$x = -3$$

8. The correct answer is 'C'

$$3a + a = 4 + 4$$
$$4a = 8$$
$$a = 2$$

9. The correct answer is 'A'

$$2x + 2 = 12$$
$$-2 \quad - 2$$
$$2x = 10$$
$$x = 5$$

10. The correct answer is 'D'

$$\frac{1}{x} = \frac{3}{2} - 1 = \frac{1}{2}$$

Therefore, $\frac{1}{x} = \frac{1}{2}$

So, $x = 2$

Algebraic Inequalities

What do I need to know?

Simplifying Inequalities:

The goal is to get x alone. Treat the inequality sign like an equal sign and perform reverse operations to get alone as you did in the prior lesson.

BUT, if you multiply or divide a negative number on both sides, you need to flip the inequality sign.

$$-3x < 21$$
$$\div -3 \qquad \div -3$$

$$x > -7$$

Notice the flipped inequality sign

Graphing Inequalities:

To graph an inequality, shade all possible numbers and the arrow if it goes on forever. If the inequality is underlined (meaning or equal to) shade in the circle on the endpoints. If not, leave an open circle on the endpoints.

x > 1   x ≥ 1

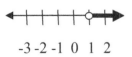

-3 -2 -1 0 1 2

-3 -2 -1 0 1 2

Example: -2x – 3 < 9

$$-2x - 3 < 9$$
$$+3 \quad +3$$

$$-2x < 12$$
$$\div -2 \quad \div -2$$

$$x > -6$$

-6 -5 -4 -3 -2 -1

Algebra
Algebraic Inequalities

1. If, $-4 \leq x < 3$, then which of the following numbers is NOT a possible value of x?

   (A) -4

   (B) -3

   (C) 2

   (D) 3

2. If $3x - 2 < 4$, which of the following is NOT a possible value of x?

   (A) -3

   (B) -1

   (C) 1

   (D) 3

3. Which of the following is a possible value of $-2x + 5 > 11$?

   (A) -4

   (B) -3

   (C) 3

   (D) 4

4. Which inequality corresponds with this diagram?

   -3 -2 -1 0 1 2

   (A) $x < 1$

   (B) $x \leq 1$

   (C) $x > 1$

   (D) $x \geq 1$

5. Which inequality corresponds with this diagram?

   -3 -2 -1 0 1 2

   (A) $x < -2 \ or \ x > 1$

   (B) $-2 < x < 1$

   (C) $-2 > x > 1$

   (D) $-2 < x > 1$

6. Which inequality is equivalent to the one below?

   $$3x + 3 \geq 12$$

   (A) $x \geq 4$

   (B) $x \leq 4$

   (C) $x \geq 3$

   (D) $x \leq 3$

7. What is the largest integer that satisfies the inequality $-15 < 3x < -6$?

   (A) -3

   (B) -2

   (C) -1

   (D) -4

8. Which of the following is the minimum
    solution to the inequality:

    $100x \geq 10000 + 3000$

    (A) 150
    (B) 140
    (C) 130
    (D) 120

9. Which inequality is represented by the
    diagram below?

    (A) $x > 1$
    (B) $x \geq 1$
    (C) $1 \leq x \leq 3$
    (D) $1 \leq x < 3$

10. Which integer(s) satisfy the inequality
    $-2 < x \leq 0$?
    (A) $-2, -1, 0$
    (B) $-2, 0$
    (C) 0
    (D) $-1, 0$

Algebraic Inequalities - Answers and Explanations

1. **The correct answer is 'D'**

   $-4 \le x < 3$

   X must be greater than or equal to -4 and less than 3.

   Since 3 is not less than 3, it is not a possible value. Remember, the inequality signs with lines under them mean less/greater than OR EQUAL to.

2. **The correct answer is 'D'**

   $3x - 2 < 4$

   $+2 \quad +2$

   $3x < 6$

   $\div 3 \quad \div 3$

   $x < 2$

   So, 3 is not a possible value.

3. **The correct answer is 'A'**

   $-2x + 5 > 11$

   $-5 \quad -5$

   $-2x > 6$

   $\div -2 \quad \div -2$

   $x < -3$ (REMEMBER, the sign swaps when you divide by a negative number)

4. **The correct answer is 'D'**

   The numbers above the 1 are shaded so it means x is greater than one. Because the circle on the 1 is also shaded, it means x is greater than 1, so $x \ge 1$.

5. **The correct answer is 'B'**

   The shading shows that x is greater than -2 and x is less than 1.

   $-2 < x < 1$

   This says, -2 is less than x which also means x is greater than negative 2.

   It also says that x is less than 1, so it is correct.

6. **The correct answer is 'C'**

   $3x + 3 \ge 12$

   $-3 -3$

   $3x \ge 9$

   $x \ge 3$

7. **The correct answer is 'A'**

   On solving the inequality 3x<-6 we get x<-2. So, the largest integer value that satisfies this strict inequality is -3(Note -2 <-2 is not correct.

8. **The correct answer is 'C'**

   $100x \ge 10000 + 3000$

   $100x \ge 13000$

   $x \ge 130$

   130 is the minimum solution.

9. **The correct answer is 'A'**

 The hollow dot at 1 represents that 1 is not included. The line continues from 1 and up to the arrow which means all numbers greater than 1 are represented.

10. **The correct answer is 'D'**

 -1 and 0 are the only integers greater than -2 and also lesser than or equal to 0.

Advanced Algebraic Equations and Inequalities

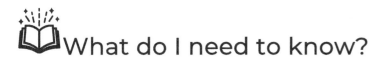

What do I need to know?

| Distributive Property | a (b + c) = ab + bc

Multiply the number outside of the parenthesis by both of the numbers inside of the parenthesis | 4(x+ 3) → 4x + 12 |
|---|---|---|
| Factoring | ab + bc = a (b + c)

Factoring is the reverse of distributing; divide out a common factor from the terms being added | 4x + 12 → 4(x+3) |

 Example: $5(2x + 6)$

$$5(2x + 6)$$
$$10x + 30$$

Advanced Algebraic Expressions and Equations

1. Which of the following is equivalent to the expression $3(4x - 5)$?

   (A) $12x - 5$

   (B) $12x + 15$

   (C) $12x - 15$

   (D) $34x - 35$

2. Which of the following is equivalent to the equation $6(4x + 2) = 3y - 2$

   (A) $24x + 14 = 3y$

   (B) $8x + 6 = y$

   (C) $8x = y$

   (D) $24x + 10 = 3y$

3. Which of the following is equivalent to the expression $16xy + 4x$?

   (A) $4xy + x$

   (B) $4(4xy + 1)$

   (C) $4x(4y + 1)$

   (D) $4x(4y + 4)$

4. Which of the following is equivalent to the equation $3y + 18 = 9x$

   (A) $3(y + 6) = 3x$

   (B) $y + 6 = 3x$

   (C) $3y = 9x + 18$

   (D) $3y = 9(x + 2)$

5. The equivalent of $\frac{a^2}{b} + \frac{b^2}{a} = 1$ is:

   (A) $a^3 + b^3 = ab$

   (B) $a^2 + b^2 = ab$

   (C) $a^2b + ab^2 = ab$

   (D) $a + b = ab$

6. Which of the following is equivalent to this expression?

   $$\frac{x}{y}\left(\frac{3x}{2} - \frac{2y}{2}\right)$$

   (A) $\frac{3x}{2y} - \frac{x}{2y}$

   (B) $\frac{3x^2y}{2} - xy^2$

   (C) $\frac{3x^2 - 2xy}{2y}$

   (D) $\frac{3x}{2y} - 1x$

7. Evaluate: $4(x^2 + 1)$

   (A) $4x^2 + 1$

   (B) $4x^2 - 4$

   (C) $4x(x - 1)$

   (D) $4x^2 + 4$

8. Which expression is the same as $3x + 9$?

   (A) $3(x + 3)$

   (B) $3(x + 9)$

   (C) $\frac{1}{3}(3x + 9)$

   (D) $\frac{1}{3}(x + 3)$

9. Solve for x:

$$3(x + 3) - 3 = 4$$

(A) -3

(B) $-\frac{2}{3}$

(C) $\frac{3}{2}$

(D) 2

10. $-3x(2y - x)$ is the same as:

(A) $(-6xy - x)$

(B) $6xy - 3x^2$

(C) $-6xy + 3x^2$

(D) $6xy + x$

1. **The correct answer is 'C'**

   $3(4x - 5) \rightarrow 3(4x) + 3(-5) = 12x - 15$.

2. **The correct answer is 'A'**

   $6(4x + 2) = 3y - 2$

   Distribute the 6

   $24x + 12 = 3x - 2$

   Add the 2 on both sides

   $24x + 14 = 3y$

3. **The correct answer is 'C'**

   $16xy + 4x$

   All terms include 4 and x, so 4x can be factored out. This would leave the first term as 4y and the second as 1.

   $4x(4y + 1)$

4. **The correct answer is 'B'**

   $3y + 18 = 9x$

   Factor out a 3 on the left side:

   $3(y + 6) = 9x$

   Divide by 3 on both sides

   $y + 6 = 3x$

5. **The correct answer is 'A'**

   $\frac{a^2(a) + b^2(b)}{ab} = 1$

   $a^3 + b^3 = ab$

6. **The correct answer is 'C'**

   $\frac{x}{y}\left(\frac{3x}{2} - \frac{2y}{2}\right)$

   $\frac{x}{y}\left(\frac{3x}{2}\right) - \frac{x}{y}\left(\frac{2y}{2}\right)$

   $\frac{3x^2}{2y} - \frac{2xy}{2y}$

   $\frac{3x^2 - 2xy}{2y}$

7. **The correct answer is 'D'**

   $4(x^2 + 1)$

   Distribute the 4

   $4x^2 + 4$

8. **The correct answer is 'B'**

   $3x + 9$

   All terms include 3, so 3 can be factored out. This would leave the first term as x and the second as 3

   $3(x + 3)$

9. **The correct answer is 'B'**

   $3(x + 3) - 3 = 4$

   $3x + 9 - 3 = 4$

   $3x + 6 = 4$

   $3x = -2$

   $x = -\frac{2}{3}$

10. **The correct answer is 'C'**

    $-3x(2y - x) =$

    $-3x(2y) - 3x(-x)$

    $= -6xy + 3x^2$

Word Problems with Algebra

What do I need to know?

On the test, you should be able to write an algebraic equation based on a word problem. To do so, look for the number that WILL change over time or with another factor and the number that WILL NOT change.

The number that WILL change goes with x since that is the variable that will make it change. The number that WILL NOT change goes on its own.

Example:

Renting a rowboat costs 5 dollars per hour with a 20 dollar set-up fee. Write an equation for the cost after x hours?

The number that WILL change with time is 5 because it is 5 dollars per hour. So, for this part you have 5x.

The number that WILL NOT change is 20 because it is a one-time fee. So, add 20.

The answer is 5x + 20.

1. The cost of renting a bicycle is S for the first 15 minutes and T for all additional minutes. What is the cost of renting a bicycle for 25 minutes in terms of S and T?

   (A) T + 10S
   (B) S + 10T
   (C) 5T + S
   (D) 25S + T

2. A dog ate an average of H treats for H days, the dog then ate an average of G treats for G days. How many treats did the dog eat in total?

   (A) 2H + 2G
   (B) HG + GH
   (C) $H^2 + G^2$
   (D) H (G + H)

3. If 3 times x is less than 8, which of the following could NOT be a value of x?

   (A) 3.25
   (B) 2.5
   (C) 2.25
   (D) 1.75

4. The cost of a go-kart ride, y, depends on the number of laps, x, driven in the go-cart, according to the formula y = 3x + 8. What is the meaning of 8 in this formula?

   (A) Every 3 laps costs 8 dollars
   (B) After 8 laps, the cost increases by 3 dollars per hour
   (C) The cost of renting a go-kart and driving 0 laps is 8 dollars
   (D) The cost of driving 3 laps in a go-kart is 8 dollars

5. A theater group is planning a production. Profit is revenue minus cost. The production will cost 3,500 dollars. The production will run for 12 nights. If tickets cost $10 each and x people are expected to attend each night. Which of the following expressions will determine the profit?

   (A) $120x + 3500$
   (B) $120 x - 3500$
   (C) $10x + 12 - 3500$
   (D) $22x - 3500$

6. Three consecutive numbers starting with x have a sum of 18. Which equation represents this situation?

(A) $x + (x + 1) + (x + 2) = 18$

(B) $x + (x + 2) + (x + 3) = 18$

(C) $x + 2x + 3x = 18$

(D) $2x + (2x + 4) + (2x + 6) = 18$

7. A ball is thrown vertically upwards to a height 'h' m from the ground. When it descends it falls on the head of a man who was passing by and who is 1.8 m tall. How many meters did the ball travel before hitting the man's head?

(A) $(h - 1.8)$ meters

(B) $(h^2 + 1 \cdot 8)$ meters

(C) $(2h + 1.8)$ meters

(D) $(2h - 1.8)$ meters

8. A bottle has volume x Liters. The volume of the bottle filled with fruit is $x / 10$ units. The rest of the bottle is filled with water. What is the volume of water in the bottle in terms of x?

(A) $9x / 10$ liters

(B) $4x / 5$ liters

(C) $2x / 3$ liters

(D) $x / 2$ liters

9. The length L of a rectangular steel window frame is twice the width w of the window. What is the perimeter of the window in terms of w?

(A) 6W

(B) 6L

(C) 3W

(D) 4L

10. During a festival, a town received an average of 10.5 hours of sunshine every day for x days. The last day the town only received 4 hours of sunshine due to the storm. How many hours of sunshine did the town receive during the festival?

(A) $10.5x + 4$

(B) $10.5 + 4x$

(C) $10.5x - 4$

(D) $10.5 - 4x$

1. **The correct answer is 'B'**

   The cost of renting a bicycle is S for the first 15 minutes and T for all additional minutes. What is the cost of renting a bicycle for 25 minutes in terms of S and T?

   First 15 minutes = S

   Each additional minute = # of additional minutes * T

   If you rent it for 25 minutes, you rent it for 10 minutes more than 15 minutes SO you pay 10T for additional minutes

   S + 10T

2. **The correct answer is 'C'**

   A dog ate an average of H treats for H days, the dog then ate an average of G treats for G days. How many treats did the dog eat in total?

   The number of treats the dog ate first is H treats x H days

   The number of treats the dog ate next is G treats x G days

   H x H + G x G = $H^2 + G^2$

3. **The correct answer is 'A'**

   If 3 times x is less than 8, which of the following could NOT be a value of x?

   3   x 3 = 9, SO it must be less than 3

   3.25 is greater than 3 so it is incorrect

4. **The correct answer is 'C'**

   The cost of a go-kart ride, y, depends on y number of laps, x, driven in the go-cart, according to the formula y = 3x + 8. What is the meaning of 8 in this formula?

   3x is the cost per lap

   8 is the start-up cost before driving any laps

   Cost = 3x + 8

   If the customer drives 0 laps, Cost = 3(0) + 8 --> Cost = 8, SO

   The cost of renting a go-kart and driving 0 laps is 8 dollars

5. **The correct answer is 'B'**

A theater group is planning a production. Profit is revenue minus cost. The production will cost 3,500 dollars. The production will run for 12 nights. If tickets cost $10 each and x people are expected to attend each night. Which of the following expressions will determine the profit?

Profit = Revenue - Cost

Revenue = (# of Nights) x (Cost of Tickets) x (# of People)

# of Nights = 12, Cost of Tickets = 10, # of People = x

Revenue = 12(10)x

Revenue = 120x

Cost = 3500

Profit = 120x – 3500

6. **The correct answer is 'A'**

The numbers immediately after x are x + 1 and x + 2.

So, the correct answer is $x + (x + 1) + (x + 2) = 18$

7. **The correct answer is 'D'**

The ball travels a height of 'h' meters going up and 'h-1.8' meters going down. So, the total distance travelled is h+h-1.8=(2h-1.8)m

8. **The correct answer is 'A'**

$1/10(x)$ is filled with fruit, $9/10 (x)$ is the rest

9. **The correct answer is 'A'**

The length of the rod will be the perimeter of the rectangular frame. Since, L=2w, the perimeter of the frame will be 2w + w +2w + w =6w In terms of L this will be 3L but it is not given among the options.

10. **The correct answer is 'A'**

The amount of hours of sunshine received in x days is 10.5x. Then, add the number that will not change with time, 4. So, the answer is 10.5x + 4

Algebra Review

1. If $x = 2$ and $y = -3$, what is

   $3x + 2y - 3$?

   (A) -3

   (B) 0

   (C) 9

   (D) 3

2. For any numbers $a@b$, $a@b =$

   $4a - 3b + 6$. What is the value of

   $-2 @ -4$?

   (A) -14

   (B) -10

   (C) 10

   (D) 14

3. $3\# = 2@$ and $6@ = 2*$

   If $\# = 2$, what is the value of $*$?

   (A) 2

   (B) 3

   (C) 6

   (D) 9

4. Simplify:

   $4a^2 + 2b - 3a^2 + 5ab + 4b - 3ab$

   (A) $a^2 + 8ab$

   (B) $a^2 + 6b + 2ab$

   (C) $3a^2b + 6b$

   (D) $a^2 + 8b + 2a$

5. Solve for x

   $$3x + 4 = -5x + 20$$

   (A) -3

   (B) -2

   (C) 2

   (D) 3

6. Solve for x

   $$\frac{x}{8} = \frac{9}{12}$$

   (A) 2

   (B) 3

   (C) 4

   (D) 6

7. If $3x + 2 < 12 + x$, which of the following numbers is NOT a possible value of x?

   (A) -5

   (B) 2

   (C) 4

   (D) 5

8. Which inequality corresponds with this diagram?

(A) - 3 < x < 1

(B) - 3 < x ≤ 1

(C) - 3 > x < 1

(D) - 3 > x ≤ 1

9. Which of the following expressions is equivalent to 3x (2x + 5)?

(A) $6x^2 + 15x$

(B) $6x^2 + 5x$

(C) $6x^2 + 5$

(D) 6x + 15

10. Which of the following is equivalent to the equation 4y + 16 = 12x?

(A) y + 4 = 3x

(B) 4(y+ 16) = 12x

(C) y+ 16 = 3x

(D) y = 3y + 4

11. Which of the following is equivalent to the expression below?

$$\frac{a}{b}\left(\frac{a^2}{ab} - \frac{b^2}{a}\right)$$

(A) $a^2 - b^2$

(B) $\frac{a^2}{b^2} - b$

(C) $\frac{a^3 - ab^2}{ab}$

(D) $\frac{a^2}{b}$

12. The cost of a movie subscription service (y), depends on the number of months (x) a person subscribes to the service according to the formula y = 8x + 12. What is the meaning of 12 in this formula?

(A) The cost per month is 12 dollars

(B) The cost of registering and paying for 0 months is 12 dollars

(C) After 8 months, the cost increases by 12 dollars

(D) The cost of renting for 8 months is 12 dollars

13. Marshall wants to start a lemonade stand. He wants to sell each glass of lemonade for $1.5. He spent a total of 20 dollars for the materials. He sells an average of x glasses a day for 4 days. Which equation represents his profit? (Profit = Revenue - Cost)

(A) 20 - 6x

(B) 6(1.5x - 20)

(C) 6x – 20

(D) 1.5 (6x + 20)

14. The cost of renting an electric scooter costs S dollars for the first 10 minutes and Y dollars for each additional minute. What is the cost of a 22-minute scooter ride?

(A) S + 12Y

(B) S + 22Y

(C) 22S + Y

(D) 12S + Y

15. If -4x - 3 < 9 which of the following numbers is a possible value of x?

(A) -2

(B) -3

(C) -4

(D) -6

Algebra Review- Answers and Explanations

1. The correct answer is 'A'

$x = 2$ and $y = -3$

$3x + 2y - 3$

$3(2) + 2(-3) - 3$

$6 - 6 - 3$

-3

2. The correct answer is 'C'

$a@b = 4a - 3b + 6$

$-2 @ -4$, SO $a = -2$, $b = -4$

$4(-2) - 3(-4) + 6$

$-8 + 12 + 6$

$4 + 6$

10

3. The correct answer is 'D'

$3\# = 2@$ and $6@ = 2*$.

$\# = 2$

$3(2) = 2@$

$6 = 2@. \rightarrow @ = 3$

$6@ = 2*$

$6(3) = 2*$

$18 = 2*$

$9 = *$

4. The correct answer is 'B'

$4a^2 + 2b - 3a^2 + 5ab + 4b - 3ab$

$a^2 + \underline{2b} + 5ab + \underline{4b} - 3ab$

$a^2 + \underline{6b} + 5ab - 3ab$

$a^2 + 6b + 2ab$

5. The correct answer is 'C'

$3x + 4 = -5x + 20$

$+ 5x \qquad + 5x$

$8x + 4 = 20$

$\quad - 4 \quad -4$

$8x = 16$

$x = 2$

6. The correct answer is "D"

$x/8 = 9/12$

$9/12 = 3/4$

$x/8 = 3/4$

$6/8 = 3/4$

$x = 6$

7. The correct answer is "D"

$3x + 2 < 12 + x$

$\quad -2 \quad - 2$

$3x < 10 + x$

$\quad - x \qquad - x$

$2x < 10$

divide by 2 on each side

$x < 5$

All number options are less than 5, except 5.

8. The correct answer is "B"

The end points are - 3 and 1

x needs to be greater than -3 and less than or equal to 1.

So, $x > -3$, $x \leq 1$

which is also

$-3 < x \leq 1$

Remember to read the inequalities from x. This says x is greater than -3 and x is less than or equal to 1.

9. The correct answer is "A"

$3x (2x + 5)$

Distribute and multiply BOTH terms by 3 x

$3x * 2x = 6 x^2$

$3x * 5 = 15x$

$6x^2 + 15x$ is correct

10. The correct answer is "A"

$4y + 16 = 12x$

Factor out 4 --> $4 (y+4) = 12x$

Divide by 4 on both sides **y + 4 = 3x**

11. The correct answer is "B"

$\frac{a}{b}\left(\frac{a^2}{ab} - \frac{b^2}{a}\right)$

$\frac{a^3}{ab^2} - \frac{ab^2}{ab}$

Cancel out the **a's**

$\frac{a^2}{b^2} - \frac{b^2}{b}$

Cancel out the **b's**

$\frac{a^2}{b^2} - b$

*Note – this is a very difficult problem, it is okay if you struggled!

12. The correct answer is "B"

$y = 8x + 12$

Remember, the 12 is the constant since it is not being multiplied by x (the number of months)

SO, if you subscribe for 0 months it would by $y = 8(0) + 12$

You would have to pay 12 dollars

13. The correct answer is "C"

Profit = Revenue - Cost

Cost: 20

Revenue: $1.5x for 4 days

SO, $1.5x * 4 = 6x$

Profit= $6x – 20$

14. The correct answer is "A"

S dollars for the first 10 minutes

Y dollars for each additional minute

Cost of the first 10 minutes + the cost of each additional minute

The scooter ride is 22 minutes, so there are 12 minutes of riding time after the 10-minute mark

S + 12Y

15. The correct answer is "A"

$-4x - 3 < 9$

$ + 3 \phantom{<} + 3$

$- 4x < 12$

Divided by -4 on each side

SO, flip the inequality

$x > - 3$. -2 is the only answer choice greater than -3

You could also solve this one by plugging in the answer choices

Geometry

Angles and Lines

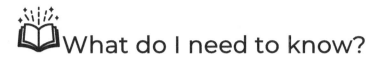 What do I need to know?

Complementary Angles	Two angles that add up to 90°	
Supplementary Angles	Two angles that add up to 180° Note: All straight lines measure 180°	
Perpendicular Lines	Two lines that intersect at a 90° angle	

For the illustrations: the complementary angles show 60° and 30°; the supplementary angles show 150° and 30°; the perpendicular lines show 90°.

Example:

Two angles are complementary, one angle is 46°, what is the measure of the other angle?

Complementary angles add up to 90°

90° − 46° = 44°

44°

Geometry

Angles and Lines

1. Two angles are complementary, one angle is 35°. What is the value of the other angle?

   (A) 50°
   (B) 55°
   (C) 145°
   (D) 150°

2. What is the value of x?

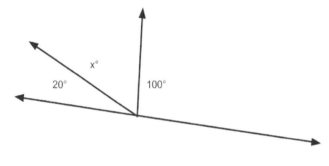

   (A) 50°
   (B) 60°
   (C) 70°
   (D) 80°

3. Two angles are supplementary, one angle is 45°. What is the value of the other angle?

   (A) 45°
   (B) 55°
   (C) 135°
   (D) 145°

4. What is the value of x?

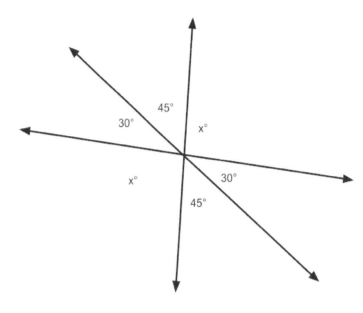

   (A) 90°
   (B) 95°
   (C) 10°
   (D) 105°

5. If x° and 30° are complementary angles and y° and 60° are complementary as well, what is the value of x°+y°?

   (A) 30°
   (B) 60°
   (C) 90°
   (D) 120°

6. Line AB and Line CD are perpendicular. What is the value of x?

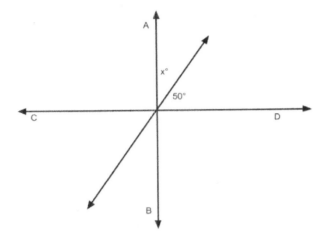

   (A) 30°
   (B) 40°
   (C) 130°
   (D) 140°

7. A 90° angle is divided into two angles in the ratio 2:3. What is the measure of the smaller angle?
   (A) 36°
   (B) 54°
   (C) 45°
   (D) 30°

8. Angles AB and BD are supplementary. The measure of angle BD is 30°. What is the measure of angle AB?
   (A) 50°
   (B) 60°
   (C) 150°
   (D) 160°

9. Angles PQ and QR are supplementary. The ratio of PQ to QR is 1:2. What is the measure of the larger angle?
   (A) 60°
   (B) 120°
   (C) 130°
   (D) 180°

10. The hour hand of a clock moves from the 12 mark to the 3 mark, from 12 noon to 3 pm. By what angle has the hour hand rotated clockwise?
   (A) 60°
   (B) 90°
   (C) 75°
   (D) 50°

1. **The correct answer is 'B'**

   If they are **complementary,** they add up to 90°.

   90° - 35° = 55°

2. **The correct answer is 'B'**

   All angles on a line will add up to 180°

   180° - 100° - 20° = 60°

3. **The correct answer is 'C'**

   If two angles are supplementary, they add up to 180°

   180°- 45°= 135°

4. **The correct answer is 'D'**

   All angles on a line add up to 180°.

   180° - 30° - 45° = 105°

5. **The correct answer is 'C'**

   Since x° and 30° are complementary so, their sum is 90°. So, x°=60°. Similarly, y° measures 30°. Therefore, x°+y°=90°.

6. **The correct answer is 'B'**

   If two lines are perpendicular, they make 90° angles.

   90° - 50° = 40°

7. **The correct answer is 'A'**

   If the ratio of the angles is 2:3 then we could also write that as 2x and 3x. We also know 2x+3x=90°. So, 5x=90° or x=18°. Therefore, the smaller angle 2x=2×18°=36°.

8. **The correct answer is 'C'.**

   Supplementary means the measures of the angles add up to 180°.

   30° + ____ = 180°

   The missing angle is 150°

9. **The correct answer is 'B'**

   If the ratio of the angles is 1:2 then we could also write that as 1x and 2x. We also know 1x+2x=180°. So, 3x=180° or x=60°. Therefore, the larger angle 2x=2×60°=120°.

10. **The correct answer is 'B'**

   90°

Polygons

What do I need to know?

Perimeter- Distance around a shape (add up all of the sides)

Area – Space inside a shape

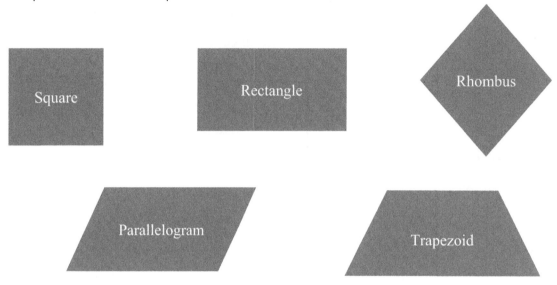

What should I memorize?

It is helpful to memorize a few area formulas.

Area of a Square, Rectangle, Parallelogram: Base x Height

Area of a Trapezoid: Average of the Bases x Height (or $\frac{Base+Base}{2}$ x Height)

Example:

What is the area of the trapezoid below?

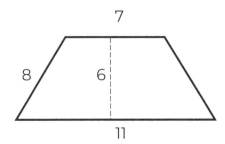

Area of a Trapezoid: Average of the Bases x Height

Base 1 = 7

Base 2 = 11

$$Average\ of\ the\ Bases = \frac{7 + 11}{2} = 9$$

Height = 6

Area = *Average of the Bases* x *Height*

Area = 6 x 9

Area = 54

Common Tricky Question Types

When a corner is cut from a rectangle as shown below, the area gets smaller, but the perimeter stays the same. The ISEE may ask you to compare perimeters, so just remember, they are the same!

6   6

10   10

1. BCEF is a square. If the length of AB is 7 and the length of BC is 4, what is the area of rectangle ACDF?

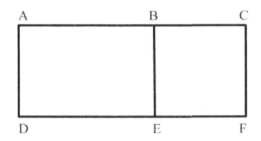

  (A) 28

  (B) 33

  (C) 44

  (D) 49

2. What kind of quadrilateral is ABCD?

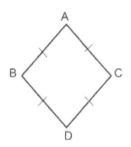

  (A) Trapezoid

  (B) Rhombus

  (C) Rectangle

  (D) Square

3. What is the area of the trapezoid below?

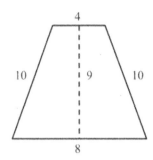

  (A) 36

  (B) 54

  (C) 60

  (D) 72

4. What is the perimeter?

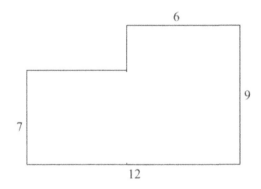

  (A) 34

  (B) 38

  (C) 42

  (D) 108

5. Which of the following is greater?

Column A
The perimeter of this shape

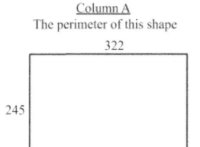

Column B
The perimeter of this shape

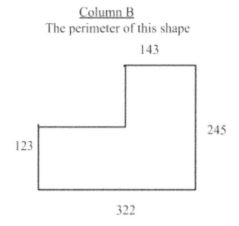

(A) Column A is greater

(B) Column B is greater

(C) Column A and B are equal

(D) The relationship cannot be determined with the information provided.

6. If a fence, must be put around a rectangular field whose dimensions are shown in the figure below, find the cost of fencing the entire field if fencing costs $10 per m.

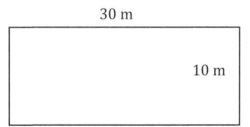

(A) $750

(B) $900

(C) $800

(D) $850

7. A square patch of field is fertile enough to produce 2 kg of vegetables per m^2. How much produce will be produced in a field with a side 5m?

(A) 45 kg

(B) 60 kg

(C) 55 kg

(D) 50 kg

8. In a chart paper factory there is a rectangular chart paper which is 2m wide and 50m long. The chart paper must be divided into 100 square chart papers of equal area. What will be the length of the side of each small chart paper?

(A) 0.5 m

(B) 0.7 m

(C) 0.9 m

(D) 1 m

9. What is the perimeter of the shape below?

2m

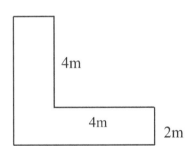

4m

4m

2m

(A) 36m

(B) 30m

(C) 24m

(D) 16m

10. What is the area of the trapezoid below?

5m

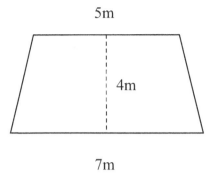

4m

7m

(A) 20m²

(B) 18m²

(C) 24m²

(D) 16m²

95

Polygons – Answers and Explanations

1. **The correct answer is 'C'**

   AB is 7 and BC is 4, so the length of the rectangle is 11. The width of the rectangle is 4 because BCEF is a square and the length of BC is 4. That means that all sides of the square are 4.

   Length: 11

   Width: 4

   Area = L x W

   11 x 4 = 44

2. **The correct answer is 'B'**

   Rhombuses have equal sides but do not just have 90-degree angles like a square

3. **The correct answer is 'B'**

   Average of the bases x the height

   $$\frac{4 + 8}{2} \times 9$$

   $$6 \times 9$$

   $$54$$

4. **The correct answer is 'C'**

   The horizontal lines on the top will add up to the distance on the bottom: 12

   The vertical lines on the left will add up to the distance on the right: 9

   12 + 12 + 9 + 9 = 42

5. **The correct answer is 'C'**

   The perimeter of a rectangle stays the same when the corner is cut out since the length and width will still add up to the same numbers.

6. **The correct answer is 'C'**

   The perimeter of the rectangular field is 2(30+10) m=80m.

   Since, fencing the field costs $10 per m, the total cost of fencing the field is $80(10)=$800

7. **The correct answer is 'D'.**

   The area of the square field is

   $5m \times 5m = 25m^2$

   There are 2kg of vegetables per m^2.

   So, 2×25 =50

8. **The correct answer is 'D'**

The area of the larger chart paper is

2m×50m=100m^2

The larger chart paper must be divided into 100 equal chart papers. So, the area of each small chart paper will be 1m^2. Now, 1m^2=1m×1m. So, the length of each side of the smaller chart paper will be 1m.

9. **The correct answer is 'C'**

$$2 + 4 + 2 + 4 + 2 + 4 + 2 + 4 = 24m$$

10. **The correct answer is 'C'**

The average of the bases of the trapezoid is

$$\frac{7+5}{2}m = 6m$$

The height of the trapezoid is 4m. So, the area of the trapezoid will be 6m×4m=24m^2.

Triangles

 ## What do I need to know?

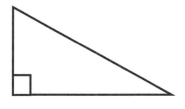

Isosceles Triangle

Two equal sides

Two equal angles

Equilateral Triangle

Three equal sides

Three equal angles (60°)

Right Triangle

Triangles with one right angle. This means sides follow special rules

Area of a Triangle: ½ base x height

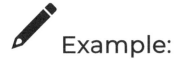 ## Example:

Find the area of the triangle below:

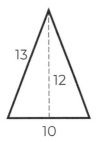

Remember the formula: ½ base x height

Base: 10

Height: 12

Side Length: 13 (Note: This is not a part of the formula so you will not use it)

½ (10) x 12

5 x 12 = **60**

Sides of Right Triangles

What do I need to know?

3 – 4 – 5 Right Triangles: These right triangles have side rations of 3:4:5.

They are similar to the triangle below:

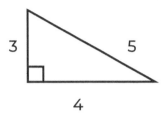

The ISEE often uses this type of triangle when you need to find a missing side length, so check to see if it is a scaled-up version of this triangle.

Example:

Find the missing side length:

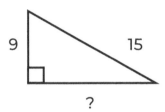

This triangle follows the 3 – 4 – 5 rule because the sides are 3 times the length of the ratio 3: 4: 5.

9 is *3* x 3

15 is *5* x 3

So, the remaining side would be *4* x 3 or **12**

If a triangle does not follow this pattern, you can use the **Pythagorean Theorem** which is on the next page. Note: This is advanced, feel free to skip this if you are not yet comfortable with the sections above

Advanced Concept:

Pythagorean Theorem

For any right triangle, $a^2 + b^2 = c^2$

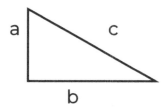

a and **b** are always the legs of the triangle and **c** is always the hypotenuse

So, if you know two lengths, you can always find the third length using this formula.

Example:

Find the missing side length:

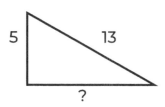

$a^2 + b^2 = c^2$

a = 5   b = ?   c = 13

$5^2 + b^2 = 13^2$

$25 + b^2 = 169$

$-25 \qquad -25$

$b^2 = 144$

$\boldsymbol{b = 12}$

1. Triangle ABC is isosceles. The length of AC is 5 and the length of BC is 2. What is the length of AB?

   (A) 2
   (B) 3
   (C) 4
   (D) 5

2. Triangle ABC is a right triangle. What is the value of x?

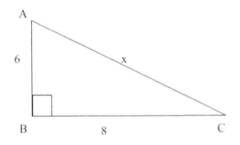

   (A) 7
   (B) 9
   (C) 10
   (D) 12

3. Triangle DEF is equilateral and has a perimeter of 24. What is the value of side DE?

   (A) 6
   (B) 8
   (C) 10
   (D) 12

4. Triangle ABC is a right triangle. What is the value of x?

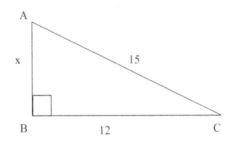

   (A) 3
   (B) 6
   (C) 9
   (D) 12

5. Triangle ABC is a right triangle. What is the value of x? *Uses Pythagorean theorem so this is an extra challenge

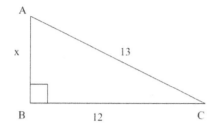

(A) 5

(B) 6

(C) 9

(D) 12

6. Triangle ABC is an isosceles triangle with the two equal sides measuring 3 cm and the third side measuring 5cm. What is the perimeter of the triangle?

(A) 10cm

(B) 12cm

(C) 11cm

(D) 9cm

7. A triangle has base equal to 6 cm and height equal to 3 cm. What is the area of the triangle(in cm^2)?

(A) 10

(B) 9

(C) 11

(D) 12

8. An equilateral triangle has one side equal to 1 cm. What is the perimeter of the triangle?

(A) 2 cm

(B) 3 cm

(C) 4 cm

(D) 5 cm

9. Find the missing length (x) of the right-triangle below.

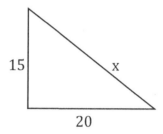

(A) 30 cm

(B) 28 cm

(C) 25 cm

(D) 7 cm

10. Find the missing length (x) of the right-angled triangle. *Uses Pythagorean theorem so this is an extra challenge

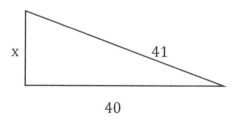

(A) 6

(B) 8

(C) 9

(D) 11

Triangles – Answers and Explanations

1. **The correct answer is 'D'**

   Since it is isosceles and the lines show which two sides are equal, we know AB and AC are equal. Since AC is 5, AB is also 5.

2. **The correct answer is 'C'**

   This is a 3-4-5 right triangle that is scaled up by 2.

   3 x 2 = 6

   4 x 2 = 8

   5 x 2 = 10

   x = 10

3. **The correct answer is 'B'**

   Because it is equilateral, all sides are equal. There are 3 sides. 24 / 3 = 8

   SO, each side is 8.

4. **The correct answer is 'C'**

   This is 3-4-5 right triangle scaled up by 3

   4 x 3 = 12

   5 x 3 = 15

   3 x 3 = 9

   x = 9

5. **The correct answer is 'A'**

   The hypotenuse (or the diagonal) is not a multiple of 5, so we cannot use the 3-4-5 rule here. We need to use the Pythagorean theorem

   $a^2 + b^2 = c^2$

   $x^2 + 12^2 = 13^2$

   $x^2 + 144 = 169$

   $ - 144 \quad - 144$

   $x^2 = 25$

   $x = 5$

6. **The correct answer is 'C'**

   Since the triangle is an isosceles triangle, two sides of it are equal in length and the third side is unequal to them. The equal sides are of length 3 cm and the third side is of length 5 cm. So, the perimeter of the triangle is 3 cm+3 cm+5 cm=11 cm.

7. **The correct answer is 'B'.**

   The area of a triangle is given by

   $\frac{1}{2} \times base \times height$

   Therefore, the area of the given triangle is

   $\frac{1}{2} \times 6\,cm \times 3\,cm = 9\,cm^2$

8. **The correct answer is 'B'.**

Since the triangle is an equilateral triangle all sides are equal and of 1 cm length, in this case. So, the perimeter of the triangle is 1 cm+ 1 cm+ 1 cm=3 cm.

9. **The correct answer is 'C'.**

By using the 3-4-5 rule for right angled triangles we see each of the given sides is 5 times 3 cm and 4 cm. So, the third side x is 5 times 5 cm=25 cm.

10. **The correct answer is 'C'**

By using the Pythagorean theorem we get $41^2 = x^2 + 40^2$ which gives $1681 = x^2 + 1600$

$1681 - 1600 = x^2$

$81 = x^2$

$9 = x$

Angles of Shapes

What do I need to know?

The Sum of the Angles Inside of a Triangle: 180°

The Sum of the Angles Inside of Quadrilateral: 360°

Example:

Find the value of x:

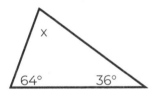

The sum of all angles inside of a triangle will always add up to 180°.

64° +36° = 100°

180° - 100° = x°

x = 80°

Similar Figures

What do I need to know?

Similar figures are the same shape, but necessarily the same size

    Here are two similar figures:

Figure A: Figure B:

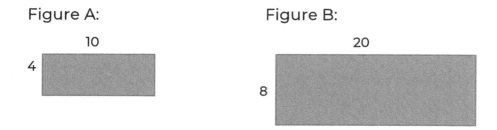

On the ISEE, you may be asked to find the missing side length of a similar figure.

Scale factor: The number the sides in the first figure can be multiplied by to get sides in the second figure

    In the example above, the sides of Figure B are 2x the sides of Figure A. So, the scale factor is 2.

Example:

The following triangles are similar. What is the value of x?

Figure A:

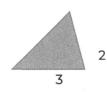

Figure B:

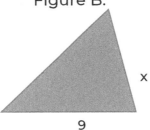

First, use the two sides you are given: 3 and 9

3 x ___ = 9

3 x 3 = 9

SO, the scale factor is 3.

Now, use that scale factor to scale up the other side.

2 x 3 = 6

So, the missing side is 6.

1. What is the value of x in this right triangle?

    (A) 40

    (B) 50

    (C) 60

    (D) 70

2. The following triangles are similar. What is the value of the missing side length?

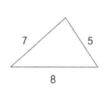 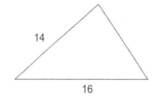

    (A) 8

    (B) 10

    (C) 12

    (D) 13

3. 3 angles of the parallelogram are given. Find the missing angle x.

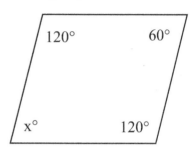

    (A) 50°

    (B) 45°

    (C) 30°

    (D) 60°

4. What is the value of y?

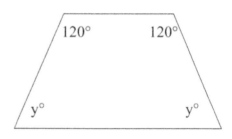

    (A) 60

    (B) 70

    (C) 90

    (D) 120

5. The following triangle is equilateral. What is the value of x?

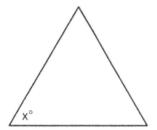

(A) 45
(B) 50
(C) 60
(D) 70

6. The following rectangles are similar. What is the value of x?

(A) 1
(B) 2
(C) 4
(D) 6

7. All the angles in a triangle are equal to 60°. Two sides are equal to 5 cm. What is the length of the third side?

(A) 3.5 cm
(B) 4 cm
(C) 4.5 cm
(D) 5 cm

8. In a 4-sided figure (quadrilateral) 3 angles are equal to 90°. What is the measure of the 4th angle?

(A) 45°
(B) 70°
(C) 90°
(D) 80°

9. The two given figures are similar. Find the missing length.

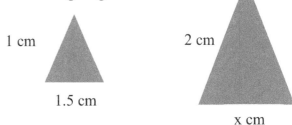

(A) 3 cm
(B) 4 cm
(C) 2 cm
(D) 1.5 cm

10. A triangle has sides of 1 cm, 2 cm and 3 cm. Another triangle similar to the first triangle has sides equal to 4 cm, 8 cm, 12 cm. What is the scale up factor for these triangles?

(A) 1
(B) 2
(C) 3
(D) 4

1. **The correct answer is 'B'**

    All interior angles will add up to 180. The lower left angle is 90 degrees because it is a right triangle.

    $90 + 40 + x = 180$

    $130 + x = 180$

    $x = 50$

2. **The correct answer is 'B'**

    Compare one of the matching sides we are giving

    $8 \rightarrow 16$

    $8 \times 2 = 16$

    You can also see that the same rule works for the other side we are given:

    $7 \times 2 = 14$

    SO, our final side corresponds to the 5 on the first triangle

    $5 \times 2 = 10$

    10

3. **The correct answer is 'D'**

    All interior angles of a quadrilateral add up to 360.

    $120 + 120 + 60 + x = 360$

    $300 + x = 360$

    $x = 60$

4. **The correct answer is 'A'**

    All interior angles of a quadrilateral add up to 360.

    $120 + 120 + y + y = 360$

    $240 + 2y = 360$

    $2y = 120$

    $y = 60$

5. **The correct answer is 'C'**

    Equilateral triangles have 3 equal angles. Al angles will add up to 180

    $3x = 180$

    $x = 60$

6. **The correct answer is 'C'**

    $3 \rightarrow 12$

    $3 \times 4 = 12$

    SO, the multiplier is 4

    $1 \times 4 = 4$

    $x = 4$

7. **The correct answer is 'D.**

    A triangle with all angles equal is an equilateral triangle, i.e. each side of is equal. Since, two sides of it are equal to 5 cm, the third side must also be equal to 5 cm.

8. **The correct answer is 'C'**

The sum of 4 angles of a quadrilateral is $360°$.

So, $3 \times 90° + x° = 360°$.

So, $x° = 90°$.

9. **The correct answer is 'A'**

Since the two triangles are similar and $1 \times 2 = 2$, so the scale up factor is 2. So, $x = 1.5 \times 2 = 3$ cm.

10. **The correct answer is 'D'**

We observe that $1 \times 4 = 4$, $2 \times 4 = 8$ and $3 \times 4 = 12$.

So, the scale up factor is 4.

Circles

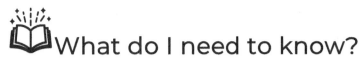

What do I need to know?

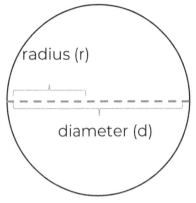

Key Formulas:

Circumference: $\pi \times d$ or $\pi \times 2 \times r$

Area: $\pi \times r^2$

Example:

A circle has an area of 25 π, what is the circumference?

First, use the given area to find the radius:

Area = $\pi \times r^2$

25 π = $\pi \times r^2$

25 = r^2

    5 = r

Second, use the radius to find the circumference:

Circumference = $\pi \times 2 \times r$

$\pi \times 2 \times 5$

Circumference =10 π

NOTE: The ISEE will almost always leave answers in terms of π

Common Tricky Question Types

The ISEE may ask you to find the area of a shaded region given a circle inscribed in a square. All you need to do, is subtract the area of the circle from the area of the square.

Area of the square – Area of the circle = Area of the shaded region

 # Example:

Find the area of the shaded region.

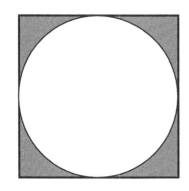

Side Length of the Square = 10   *Area of the Square* = 10 x 10 = 100

The diameter of the circle is also 10

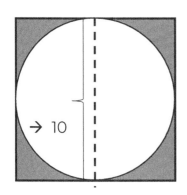

Diameter = 10

Radius = 5

Area of the Circle = $\pi \times r^2$ → $\pi \times 5^2 = 25\,\pi$

Area of the Square – Area of the Circle =

100 - 25 π

This is your answer because the ISEE will always leave answers in terms of π

1. What is the area of a circle with a diameter of 4?

   (A) 2 π

   (B) 4 π

   (C) 10 π

   (D) 16 π

2. The area of a circle is 16 π, what is the circumference?

   (A) 2 π

   (B) 4 π

   (C) 8 π

   (D) 10 π

3. The diameter of a circle is 6. What is the circumference?

   (A) 3 π

   (B) 4 π

   (C) 6 π

   (D) 12 π

4. Below is a circle inscribed in a square. What is the area of the shaded region?

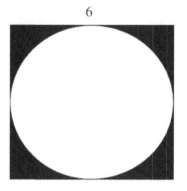

6

   (A) 36 - 9 π

   (B) 36 - 3 π

   (C) 144 - 36 π

   (D) 64 - 36π

5. Two equivalent circles are inscribed in a rectangle. What is the area of circle A?

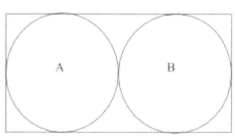

16

   (A) 4 π

   (B) 8 π

   (C) 12 π

   (D) 16 π

6. The area of a circle is 49π. What is its diameter?

(A) 7 cm

(B) 14 cm

(C) 9 cm

(D) 16 cm

7. The area of the base of a cake is 36π units^2. The cake is cut into quarters. What is the area of the base of one of the quarters?

(A) 8 π

(B) 9 π

(C) 10 π

(D) 12 π

8. A circle has circumference equal to 8 π units. What is its radius?

(A) 3

(B) 2

(C) 4

(D) 16

9. A circular tent has base radius 2m. What is the area of the base of the tent?

(A) 2π

(B) 4 π

(C) 8 π

(D) 16 π

10. A circle is inscribed inside a square of side 12 m. What is the area of the shaded region?

(A) 156-36 π

(B) 144-6 π

(C) 156-12 π

(D) 144-36 π

1. The correct answer is 'B'

The diameter is 4, so the radius is 2.

Area = πr^2

$\pi 2^2$

4π

2. The correct answer is 'C'

Area = πr^2

$r^2 = 16$

$r = 4$

Circumference = $2\pi r$

$C = 2\pi 4$

$C = 8\pi$

3. The correct answer is 'C'

Circumference = $2 \pi r$ OR πd

2 x radius = diameter

Diameter = 6

Diameter x π = Circumference

6π

4. The correct answer is 'A'

Area of the square - Area of the circle = Area of the shaded region

The Area of the square is 36 since one side length is 6.

The diameter of the circle is 6, so the radius is 3.

A = π r ^2

A = π 3 ^2

A = 9 π

Area of the square - Area of the circle = Area of the shaded region

36 - 9 π

5. The correct answer is 'D'

The diameter of each circle is 8 because the length across both of them is 16.

So, the radius of circle A is 4.

Area is π r ^2

π 4 ^2

π 16

6. The correct answer is 'B'

The area of circle of radius r is πr^2. Here, $\pi r^2 = 49\,\pi$. So, $r^2 = 49$ or r=7. So, diameter=2×7=14 units.

7. The correct answer is 'B'

A quarter of $36\,\pi = \frac{1}{4} \times 36\pi = 9\pi$.

8. The correct answer is 'C'

The circumference of a circle of radius r is $2\,\pi r$. So, in the given circle r=4.

9. The correct answer is 'B'

The area of the tent base is $2^2\pi = 4\,\pi$.

10. The correct answer is 'D'

The area of the square is 12×12=144 square units. The area of the circle is $\pi(6^2) = 36\pi$ square units since, the diameter of the circle is of equal length to the side of the square i.e. 12 units. So, the radius of the circle is 6 units. Therefore, the area of the shaded region=144-36 π

3D Shapes

 What do I need to know?

Surface Area: The total area of all sides of the shape. Find the area of each of the sides and add them up.

Volume of Any Prism: Area of the Base x Height

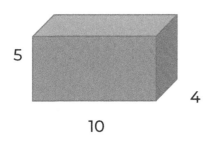

Area of the Rectangle Base x Height

4 x 10   x   5

4 x 10 x 5 = 200

Area of the Circle Base x Height

4 x 4 x π   x   10

4 x 4 x π x 10   = 160 π

 Common Tricky Question Types:

The ISEE often asks you to convert between the surface area and volume of a cube. Since cubes have 6 equal sides, you can just learn these two formulas to solve those common tricky questions.

Volume of a Cube = side x side x side or s^3

Surface Area of a Cube = 6 x side x side or $6s^2$

Example:

A cube has a surface area of 150 cm². What is the volume?

First, find the side length using the given surface area:

Surface Area of a Cube = 6 x side x side or $6s^2$

$$150 = 6 \times s \times s$$
$$\div 6 \qquad \div 6$$
$$25 = s \times s$$
$$5 = s$$

Now, find the volume using the side length:

Volume of a Cube = side x side x side or s^3

$$\text{Volume} = 5 \times 5 \times 5$$
$$\text{Volume} = 125 \text{ cm}^2.$$

For questions 1 and 2 use the shape below:

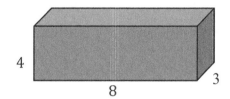

1. What is the volume of the shape above?

    a. 48

    b. 64

    c. 96

    d. 120

2. What is the surface area of the shape above?

    a. 96

    b. 120

    c. 136

    d. 148

3. The circle at the base of a cylinder has an area of 54π square units. The height of the cylinder is 3 units. Find the volume of the cylinder.
    (A) 54 π
    (B) 108 π
    (C) 136 π
    (D) 162 π

4. A cube has a surface area of 96 cm². What is the volume of the cube?
    (A) 16 cm²
    (B) 64 cm²
    (C) 80 cm²
    (D) 96 cm²

5. The volume of a cube is 125 cm². What is the surface area?
    (A) 25 cm²
    (B) 100 cm²
    (C) 125 cm²
    (D) 150 cm²

6. The surface area of a cube is 24. What is the volume?
    (A) 4
    (B) 8
    (C) 16
    (D) 24

7. A cube has a volume of 216. What is the surface area?
    (A) 36
    (B) 144
    (C) 216
    (D) 225

8. What is the surface area of a rectangular prism with a height of 4, a base of 2 and a width of 6?

   (A) 12

   (B) 48

   (C) 88

   (D) 96

9. A cube has a volume of 27. What is the surface area?

   (A) 9

   (B) 36

   (C) 54

   (D) 81

10. A cube has a volume of 64. What is the surface area?

   (A) 96

   (B) 108

   (C) 144

   (D) 164

1. The correct answer is 'C'

$V = b \times w \times h$

$V = 8 \times 3 \times 4$

$V = 96$

2. The correct answer is 'C'

To find surface area, add up the area of all of the faces.

There are two rectangles with a base of 3 and a height of 4. Area of one = 12

There are two rectangles with a base of 8 and a height of 3. Area of one = 24

There are two rectangles with a base of 4 and a height of 8. Area of one = 32

SA = 12+12+24+24+32+32

SA = 136

3. The correct answer is 'D'

The volume of any prism is the area of the base x height.

Area of base = $54\,\pi$

Height = 3

$54\,\pi \times 3 = 162\,\pi$

4. The correct answer is 'B'

$SA = 6 \times s \times s$

$96 = 6 \times s \times s$

96/ 6 = 16 SO, s x s = 16

s = 4

Volume= $s \times s \times s$

Volume = 16 x 4

Volume = 64

5. The correct answer is 'D'

$V = s \times s \times s$

$125 = s \times s \times s$

$125 = 5 \times 5 \times 5$

s= 5

$SA = s \times s \times 6$

$SA = 5 \times 5 \times 6$

$SA = 25 \times 6$

$SA = 150$

6. The correct answer is 'B'

Surface Area = (Area of the square) x 6

24 = (Area of the square) x 6

24 = (4) x 6

SO, Area of the square is 4

Side of the square is 2

Volume = side x side x side

Volume= 2 x 2 x 2

Volume = 8

7. The correct answer is 'C'

$V = s \times s \times s$

$216 = s \times s \times s$

$216 = 6 \times 6 \times 6$

s= 6

$SA = s \times s \times 6$

$SA = 6 \times 6 \times 6$

$SA = 36 \times 6$

$SA = 216$

8. **The correct answer is 'C'**

To find surface area, add up the area of all of the faces.

There are two rectangles with a base of 2 and a height of 4. Area of one = 8.

There are two rectangles with a base of 2 and a height of 6. Area of one = 12

There are two rectangles with a base of 6 and a height of 4. Area of one = 24

SA = 8+8+12+12+24+24

SA = 88

9. **The correct answer is 'C'**

$V = s \times s \times s$

$27 = s \times s \times s$

$27 = 3 \times 3 \times 3$

$s = 3$

$SA = s \times s \times 6$

$SA = 3 \times 3 \times 6$

$SA = 9 \times 6$

SA = 54

10. **The correct answer is 'A'**

Volume = 64

Volume = side x side x side

64 = side x side x side

64 = 4 x 4 x 4

Surface area = 6 x (area of each square)

Area of each square is 4 x 4 = 16

Surface area = 6 x 16 = 96

Nets

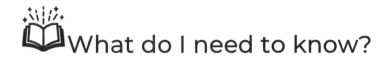

What do I need to know?

Net: A net is what a 3D shape would look like if it were folded out flat.

To choose the correct net of a 3D shape, look at the 3D shape and find patterns and rules. You may look at the number of sides or the relationship between the patterns on the shape. Then, find the net in the answer choices that follows the same rule.

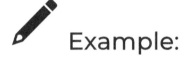 Example:

Which is a possible net for this cube?

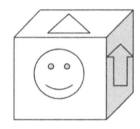

(A)

(B)

(C)

(D)

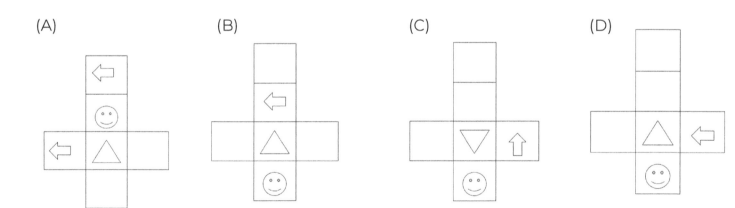

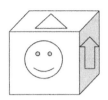

Look at the cube and determine the rules:

The base of the triangle must connect to the top of the smiley face

The arrow must point toward the triangle

The only two options with the base of the triangle connecting to the smiley face are these two:

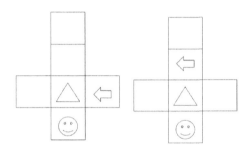

The only one of these with the arrow pointing toward the triangle is

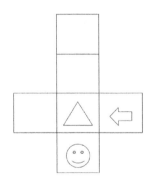

So, D is the answer

1. Which of the following could be a net for the cube?

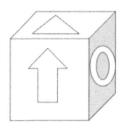

(A)

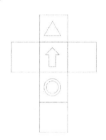

(B)

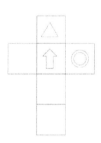

(C)

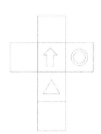

(D)

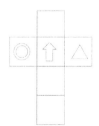

2. Which of the following could be a net for this cube?

(A)

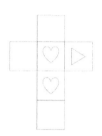

(B)

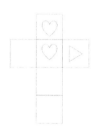

(C)

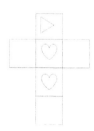

(D)

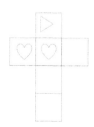

3. Which of the following could be a net of this cube?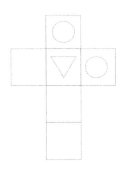

(A)

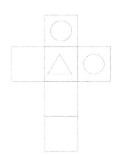

(B)

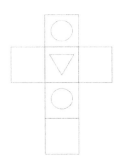

(C)

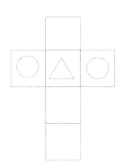

(D)

4. Which of the following shapes corresponds with the net below?

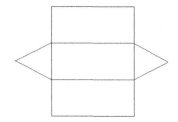

(A)

(B)

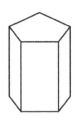

(C)

(D)

5. Which of the following shapes corresponds with the net below?

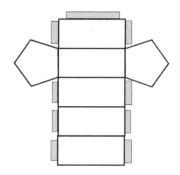

(A)

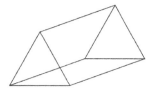

(B)

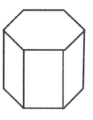

(C)

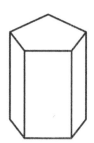

(D)

6. Which of the following nets corresponds with the shape below?

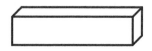

(A)

(B)

(C)

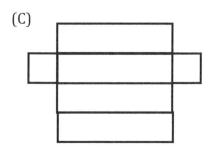

(D)

7. Which of the following shapes best corresponds with the net below?

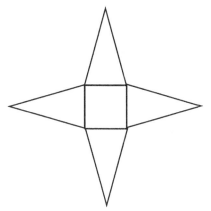

(A)

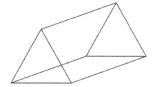

(B)

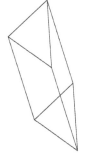

(C)

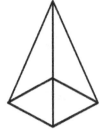

(D)

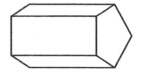

8. Which of the following could be a net for the cube?

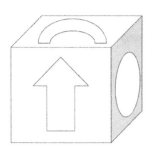

(A)

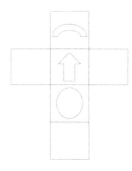

(B)

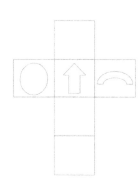

(C)

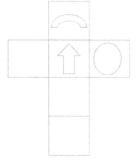

(D)

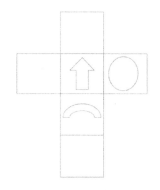

9. Which of the following shapes best corresponds with the net below?

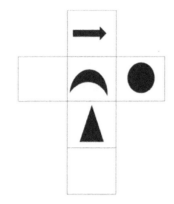

(A)

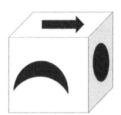

(B)

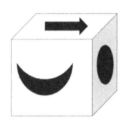

(C)

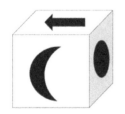

(D)

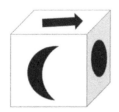

10. Which of the following shapes best corresponds with the net below?

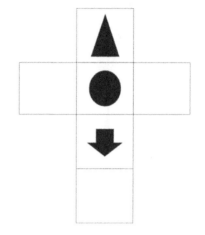

(A)

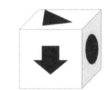

(B)

(C)

(D)

Nets- Answers and Explanations

1. **The correct answer is 'B'**

    The arrow points to the base of the triangle (A and B).

    The circle is next to the upward arrow (only B).

2. **The correct answer is 'D'**

    The sides of the hearts are each next to each other (only D).

3. **The correct answer is 'B'**

    The tip of the triangle points to a circle (B and C).

    There is a circle along the diagonal side of the triangle (only B).

4. **The correct answer is 'D'**

    The base has 3 sides.

5. **The correct answer is 'C'**

    The base has 5 sides.

6. **The correct answer is 'C'**

    The shape has 4 rectangular sides and one square on each end.

7. **The correct answer is 'C'**

    The shape a square base and 4 triangular sides.

8. **The correct answer is 'C'**

    The arrow points into the arch. The circle is alongside the arrow.

9. **The correct answer is 'A'**

    The arrow sits on top of the arch of the moon. The circle is next to one point of the moon.

10. **The correct answer is 'B'**

    The arrow points away from the circle.

Coordinate Planes

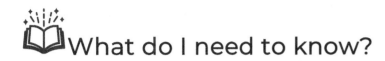
Coordinate points

Coordinate points are written as (x, y). The x value is on the horizontal axis and the y value is on the vertical axis.

To graph a point, first, find the x value on the horizontal line, then move the point up or down to reach the y value.

The point that is graphed is (4, 3). The point is in line with the 4 on the x axis and the 3 on the y axis.

Transformations

A transformation occurs when a shape is moved from one point to another. It is helpful to learn the names of these transformations shown below.

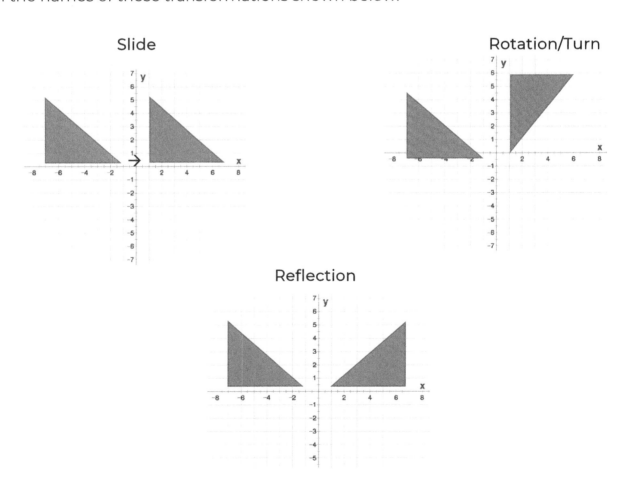

132

Example:

Marshall is drawing a rectangle. Where should he put the last vertex?

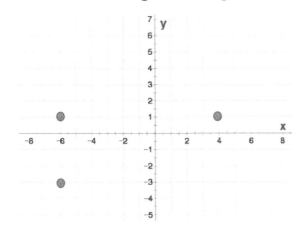

First, draw in the shape and identify the final point.

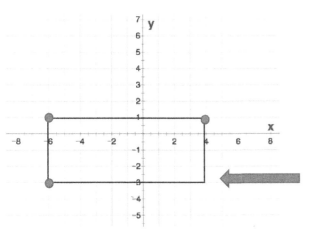

Next, determine the coordinates of the final point.

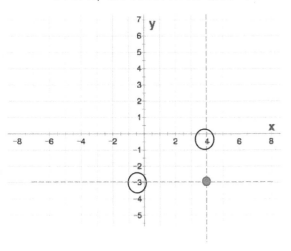

The point lines up with 4 on the x axis and -3 on the y axis. So, the point is (4, -3).

133

1. What type of transformation was performed?

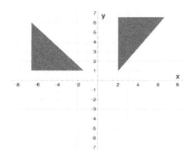

(A) Slide

(B) Rotation

(C) Reflection

(D) Shift

2. At which point does this line hit the y-axis?

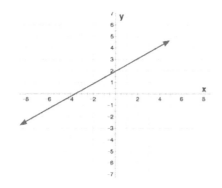

(A) (2, 0)

(B) (0,2)

(C) (-4, 0)

(D) (0, -4)

3. Karla is drawing a parallelogram. She drew three of the vertices below. Where should she draw the fourth vertex?

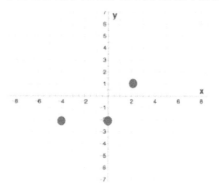

(A) (-2, 1)

(B) (-6, 1)

(C) (2, -2)

(D) (2, -1)

4. What type of transformation was performed?

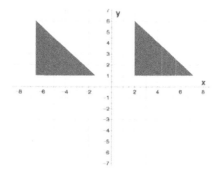

(A) Rotation

(B) Turn

(C) Slide

(D) Reflection

5. Maria is drawing a square. Where should she put the last vertex?

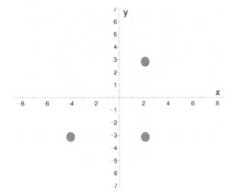

(A) (- 4, 3)

(B) (3, - 4)

(C) (8, 3)

(D) (- 6, 3)

6. At which point does the line below touch the x-axis?

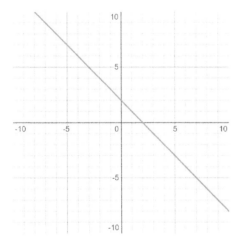

(A) (2,0)

(B) (0,2)

(C) (1,0)

(D) (0,1)

7. What type of transformation was performed below?

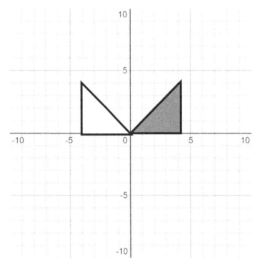

(A) Translation

(B) Rotation

(C) Reflection

(D) No change

8. Celia moves a point at the origin (0, 0) up 5 units. What are the coordinates of her new point?

(A) (2.5, 0)

(B) (0, 2.5)

(C) (5, 0)

(D) (0, 5)

135

9. Helen is drawing a rectangle and marking its vertices first. What will be the coordinates of the 4th vertex?

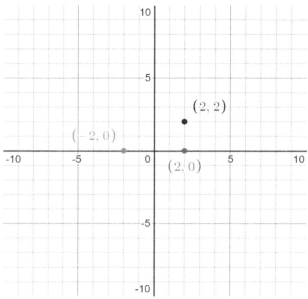

    (A) (0, 2)

    (B) (0, -2)

    (C) (-2, -2)

    (D) (-2, 2)

10. Hector moved a point 5 units to the right from the origin (0, 0). What are the coordinates of his new point?

    (A) (2.5, 0)

    (B) (0, 2.5)

    (C) (5, 0)

    (D) (0, 5)

1. **The correct answer is 'B'**

   This is a rotation because the first triangle was rotated 90 degrees

2. **The correct answer is 'B'**

   Points are written as (x, y)

   This point hits at x = 0, y = 2 which is (0, 2)

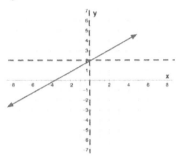

3. **The correct answer is 'A'**

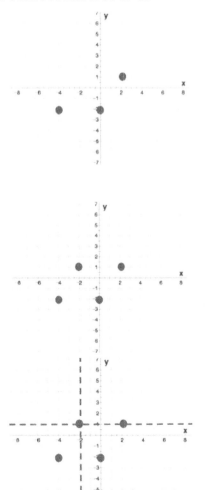

4. **The correct answer is 'C'**

   This is a slide because the triangle was shifted over and the orientation did not change

5. **The correct answer is 'A'**

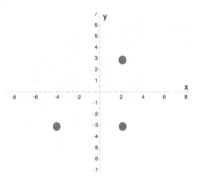

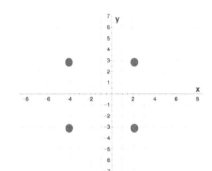

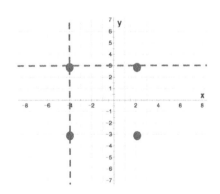

6. **The correct answer is 'A'**

On the x-axis all points have y-coordinate 0. Also, the x-intercept of the line is 2 units over. So, the answer is (2,0).

7. **The correct answer is 'C'**

The first triangle is reflected over the y axis to make the second triangle.

8. **The correct answer is 'D'**

If Celia moves the point 5 units above the origin, she travel 0 distance along the x-axis and 5 units along the y-axis. So, the point is (0, 5)

9. **The correct answer is 'D'**

(-2, 2) is the point that will complete this rectangle.

10. **The correct answer is 'C'.**

If Hector travels 5 units to the right of the origin, he travels 5 units along the x-axis and 0 units along the y-axis. So, the answer is (5, 0)

Slope

What do I need to know?

Slope refers to the steepness of a line. The farther the slope is from 0, the steeper the line.

Slope is one of those advanced math concepts that you may not learn in school before the ISEE. To simply find a slope, learn these two methods. If you feel ready for a more advanced understanding, read the advanced section as well.

1. Find the slope given an equation

    Make the equation equal y and simplify the other side. The slope will be next to the x.

    y = SLOPE (x) + Y-INTERCEPT

    y = 3x + 2

    Slope = 3

2. Find the slope given two points

    Use the formula:

    $$\frac{y_2 - y_1}{x_2 - x_1}$$

    Given (2, 1) and (4, 2)

    $$\text{Slope} = \frac{4 - 2}{2 - 1}$$

    Slope = 2

Example:

Which of the following is greater?

<u>Column A</u>

The slope of

the line

$y - x = 3x - 1$

<u>Column B</u>

The slope of

the line containing:

(2, -2) (5, 1)

(A) Column A is greater

(B) Column B is greater

(C) Column A and B are equal

(D) The relationship cannot be determined with the information given.

<u>Column A</u>

First, make the equation = y

$y - x = 3x - 1$

$+ x \qquad + x$

$y = 4x - 1$

Slope = 4

<u>Column B</u>

(2, -2) (5, 1)

$\frac{y_2 - y_1}{x_2 - x_1} \rightarrow \frac{1 - (-2)}{5 - 2} \rightarrow \frac{3}{3} = 1$

Slope = 1

Column A is greater.

Advanced Concept

Finding Slope from a Graph

$$\frac{Rise}{Run} \text{ or } \frac{Change \; in \; y}{Change \; in \; x}$$

1. Identify two points on the graph:

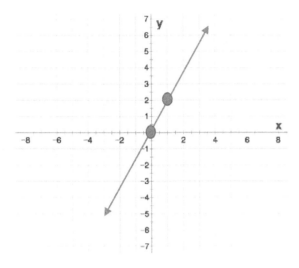

2. Count the change in y or the rise from one point to the next.

3. Count the change in x or the "run" from one point to the.

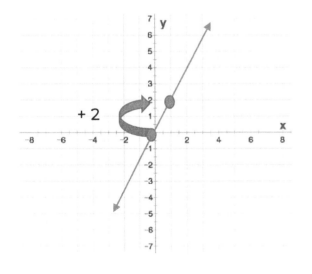

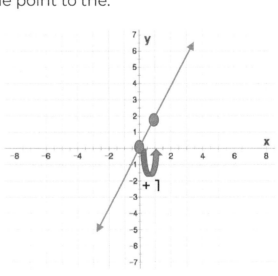

3. Slope = $\frac{Rise}{Run}$ or $\frac{Change \; in \; y}{Change \; in \; x}$ → Slope = $\frac{2}{1}$ or 2

Advanced Concept

Slope of Parallel and Perpendicular Lines

To find the slope of a **parallel line,** use the same slope as that of the original line.

To find the slope of a **perpendicular line,** flip the slope and multiply by -1.

 Example:

What is the slope of a line perpendicular to the line y = 3x – 1?

$$y = 3x - 1$$

Original Slope = 3

To find the slope of the perpendicular, flip it and multiply by – 1.

Original Slope = 3 or $\frac{3}{1}$

Flip it→ $\frac{1}{3}$

Multiply by – 1 → - 1/3

1. What is the slope of the line 4y + 2 = 3x - 6?

   (A) $\frac{3}{4}$

   (B) $\frac{4}{3}$

   (C) 3

   (D) 4

2. What is the slope of the line 3y + 2x = 4?

   (A) -2

   (B) $-\frac{2}{3}$

   (C) $\frac{2}{3}$

   (D) 3

3. A line has an equation of y = -2 x + 4. What is the slope of the line?

   (A) -4

   (B) -2

   (C) 2

   (D) 4

4. The equation of a line is 3y - 9 x = 6. What is the slope?

   (A) -9

   (B) -3

   (C) 3

   (D) 9

5. The equation of a line is 4y - 3x = 12. What is the slope?

   (A) -3

   (B) $\frac{1}{4}$

   (C) $\frac{3}{4}$

   (D) 3

6. Which of the following is greater?

Column A	**Column B**
The slope of	The slope of
the line	the line containing:
y = 4x + 2	(3, 2) (4, -4)

   (A) Column A is greater

   (B) Column B is greater

   (C) Column A and B are equal

   (D) The relationship cannot be determined with the information given.

7. Which of the following is greater?

Column A

The slope of
the line
$2y = -6x + 4$

Column B

The slope of
the line containing:
$(0, 3)$ $(1, 8)$

(A) Column A is greater

(B) Column B is greater

(C) Column A and B are equal

(D) The relationship cannot be
    determined with the information
    given.

8. Which of the following is greater?

Column A

The slope of
the function
$3y = 9x + 6$

Column B

The slope of
the line containing:
$(2, 5)$ $(4, 2)$

(A) Column A is greater

(B) Column B is greater

(C) Column A and B are equal

(D) The relationship cannot be
    determined with the information
    given

9. In which function does y increase at the
   greatest value as the value of x increases?

(A)

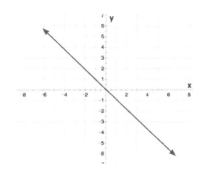

(B)

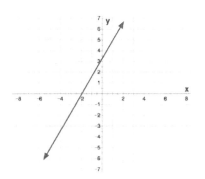

(C)

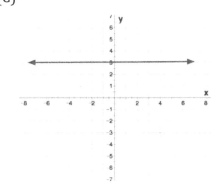

(D)

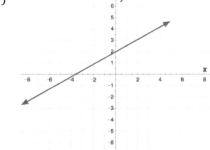

10. Which of the following is the equation of the line perpendicular to the line below at the point (2, 3)?

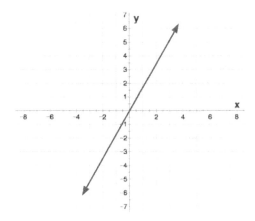

(A) $y = -\frac{1}{2}x + 4$

(B) $y = -\frac{1}{2}x - 4$

(C) $y = 2x + 4$

(D) $y = 2x$

Slope – Answers and Explanations

1. The correct answer is 'A'

$4y + 2 = 3x - 6$

$\quad - 2 \qquad - 2$

$\underline{4y} = \underline{3x} - \underline{8}$

$\;4 \quad\; 4 \quad\; 4$

$y = \underline{3}\,x - 2$

$\quad\; 4$

$y = mx + b$ - m is slope

$\underline{3} = $ slope

4

2. The correct answer is 'B'

$3y + 2x = 6$

$\quad - 2x \quad -2x$

$\underline{3y} = \underline{-2x + 6}$

$\;3 \qquad 3 \quad 3$

$y = \underline{-2}\,x + 2$

$\qquad\; 3$

3. The correct answer is 'B'

Equation of a line:

$y = $ SLOPE (x) + Y-INTERCEPT

$y = -2\,x + 4$

Slope = - 2

4. The correct answer is 'C'

$Y = $ SLOPE (x) + Y-INTERCEPT

$3y - 9\,x = 6$

Change the equation to make it = y so you can identify the slope

$3y - 9\,x = 6$

$\quad + 9x \quad + 9x$

$3y = 9x + 6 \;\rightarrow$ Divide everything by 3

$\underline{3y} = \underline{9x + 6}$

$\;3 \quad\; 3 \quad\; 3$

$y = 3x + 2$

Slope = 3

5. The correct answer is 'C'

$Y = $ SLOPE (x) + Y-INTERCEPT

$4y - 3x = 12$

Change the equation to make it = y so you can identify the slope

$4y - 3x = 12$

$\quad + 3x \quad + 3x$

$4y = 3x + 12 \;\rightarrow$ Divide everything by 4

$\underline{4y} = \underline{3x} + \underline{12}$

$\;4 \quad\; 4 \quad\; 4$

$y = \underline{3x} + 3$

$\qquad 4$

Slope = ¾

6. **The correct answer is 'A'**

   Column A

   y = 4x + 2

   Slope = 4

   Column B

   $$\frac{-4-2}{4-3} = -\frac{6}{1}$$

   Slope = -6

   Column A is greater. With these, you are often just looking for one that is positive and one that is negative. So, if you are struggling to find the slope for two points, use the other. Choose the one that is positive as your answer.

7. **The correct answer is 'B'**

   Column A

   Divide by 2 on both sides

   y = - 3 x + 2

   Slope = -3

   Column B

   $$\frac{8-3}{1-0} = \frac{5}{1}$$

   Slope = 5

   Column B is greater. With these, you are often just looking for one that is positive and one that is negative. So, if you are struggling to find the slope for two points, use the other. Choose the one that is positive as your answer.

8. **The correct answer is 'A'**

Column A	Column B
3y = 9x + 6	(2, 5) (4, 2)

   Column A

   $$\frac{3y = 9x + 6}{3}$$

   y = 3x + 2

   Slope = 2

   Column B

   $$\frac{2-5}{4-2} = -\frac{3}{2}$$

9. **The correct answer is 'B'**

   For grid A, y decreases as x increases

   For grid B, as x goes up 1, y goes up 2

   For grid C, y stays the same as x increases

   For grid D, as x goes up 2, y goes up 1

   Therefore, this one increases at the highest rate. It is also visually steepest which is how you can know quickly.

10. The correct answer is 'A'

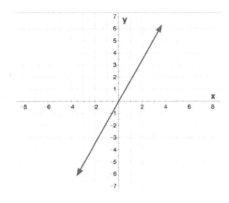

The slope of this line is 2/1. SO, the slope of the perpendicular line is - 1/2.

The y-intercept (or b in y = mx + b), would be positive because a sketch would look something like this:

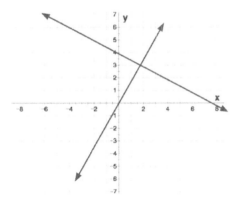

Of the two options with -1/2 as the slope, only one has a positive y-intercept.

So, y = - 1/2 x + 4 is the answer

1. BCEF is a square. If the length of AC is 10 and the length of DE is 7, what is the area of rectangle ACDF?

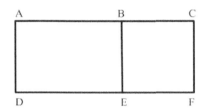

(A) 30

(B) 40

(C) 50

(D) 70

2. The triangle below is a right triangle. What is the length of AB?

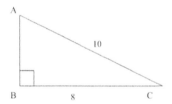

(A) 3

(B) 4

(C) 6

(D) 8

3. Which of the following is greater?

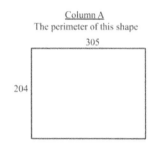 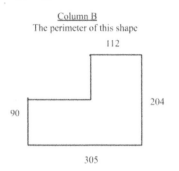

(A) Column A is greater

(B) Column B is greater

(C) Column A and Column B are equal

(D) The relationship cannot be determined with the information given.

4. The two angles are complementary, one angle is 55°. What is the value of the other angle?

(A) 25

(B) 35

(C) 45

(D) 55

5. What is the slope of the line 5y - 3 = 4x + 7?

(A) 4/5

(B) 5/4

(C) 4

(D) 5

6. Which of the following could be a net of this cube?

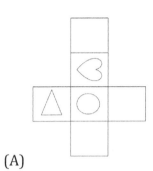

(A)

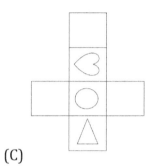

(C)

(B)

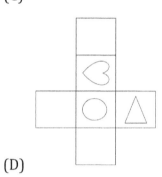

(D)

7. What is the value of x in this right triangle?

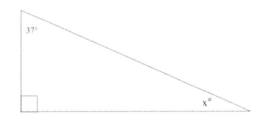

(A) 37

(B) 47

(C) 53

(D) 63

8. Lucas is drawing a trapezoid. Where should he put the last vertex?

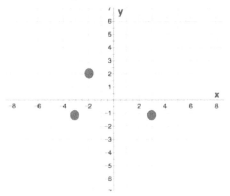

   (A) (- 2, - 2)

   (B) (- 2, 1)

   (C) (2, 2)

   (D) (5, 2)

9. The following triangles are similar. What is the value of the missing side length?

   (A) 12

   (B) 16

   (C) 18

   (D) 19

10. What type of transformation was performed?

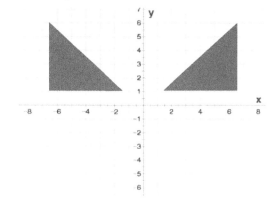

   (A) Rotation

   (B) Slide

   (C) Reflection

   (D) Turn

11. Which of the follow is greater?

Column A	Column B
$y + 5 = 3x + 6$	(2, 6) (-1, 7)

   (A) Column A is greater

   (B) Column B is greater

   (C) Column A and Column B are equal

   (D) The relationship cannot be determined from the information given

12. The volume of a cube is 125. What is the surface area?

   (A) 100

   (B) 125

   (C) 150

   (D) 175

13. What is the value of x?

    (A) 35

    (B) 45

    (C) 55

    (D) 90

14. What is the area of the shaded region?

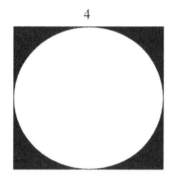

    (A) $16 - 4\pi$

    (B) $16 - 2\pi$

    (C) $20 - 4\pi$

    (D) $16 - 8\pi$

15. Which of the following is the equation of the line perpendicular to the line below a point (2, 0)?

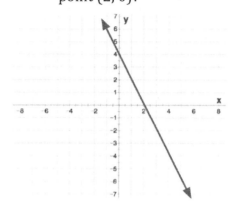

    (A) $y = -2x - 1$

    (B) $y = -2x + 5$

    (C) $y = 1/2 x + 5$

    (D) $y = 1/2 x - 1$

Geometry Review – Answers and Explanations

1. The correct answer is 'A'

If AC is 10 and DE is 7, that means that EF is 3. So, the side length of the square is 3. The area would be the side length of the square CF x the length of the rectangle 10.

3 x 10 = 30

2. The correct answer is 'C'

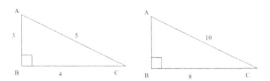

This is a 3:4:5 right triangle so it is an enlarged version of the one on the right. Each side is 2 x the one on the right.

4 x 2 = 8

5 x 2 = 10

3 x 2 = 6

SO, the last side is 6

3. The correct answer is 'C'

The perimeter of a rectangle stays the same when the corner is cut out since the length and width will still add up to the same numbers.

4. The correct answer is 'B'

Two complementary angles add up to 90 degrees.

90-55 = 35

35 = x

5. The correct answer is 'A'

5y - 3 = 4x + 7

+ 3   + 3

5y = 4x + 10

÷5 ÷5 ÷5

y = 4/5 x + 2

y = (slope)x + y intercept

Slope = 4/5

6. The correct answer is "B"

First look for rules:

Top of the heart must connect to the circle

Side of the heart must line up with the side of the triangle

Triangle must point to the circle

7. The correct answer is "C"

All angles in a triangle add up to 180.

So, 180 - 90 - 37 = 53

8. The correct answer is "C"

(x, y) x = 2, y= 2

(2, 2)

9. The correct answer is "B"

6 x 4 = 24

5 x 4 = 20

4 x 4 = 16

10. The correct answer is "C"

The triangle is reflected over the y-axis, so it is a reflection.

11. The correct answer is "A"

Column A

$y + 5 = 3x + 6$

$\quad - 5 \quad\quad -5$

$y = 3x + 1$

Slope = 3

Column B

$(2, 6) \ (-1, 7)$

$\dfrac{y_2 - y_1}{x_2 - x_1} \rightarrow \dfrac{7 - 6}{-1 - 2} = -\dfrac{1}{3}$

Column A is greater

12. The correct answer is "C"

Volume = side x side x side

$125 = 5 \times 5 \times 5$

Surface area =

6 (side x side) OR volume of one face x 6

6 (5 x 5)

6 (25)

150

13. The correct answer is "B"

All angles in a quadrilateral add up to 360.

360 - 135 - 135 = 90

$x + x = 90$

$x = 45$

14. The correct answer is "A"

Area of the square - Area of the circle

Area of the square = 4 x 4 = 16

Area of the circle = $\pi\, r^2$

The diameter of the circle is 4 because it is the same as the side of the square. SO, the radius is 2

Area = $\pi\, 2^2 = 4\,\pi$

Area of the square - Area of the circle

16 - 4 π

15. The correct answer is "D"

The slope of the line is - 2

SO, the slope of the perpendicular line would be the negative reciprocal

So, 1/2

The two options with 1/2 as the slope are:

y= 1/2 x + 5

y = 1/2 x - 1

Remember, y = (slope)x + y-intercept

If we sketch the line, starting at point (2, 0) we can guess where the line would hit the y-axis

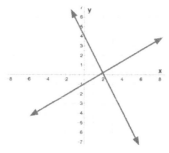

We can tell from the sketch that it would hit the y-axis at -1, SO

y = 1/2 x -1 is our answer

Data and Probability

Charts and Graphs

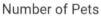 What do I need to know?

A **pie chart** shows the data as a percentage of the whole.

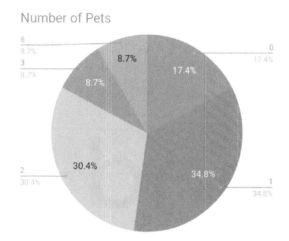

So, 30.4% of people had 2 pets and 34.8% of people had 1 pet.

A **bar graph** shows the number of people who gave each answer. Pay close attention to the labels to interpret the chart correctly.

Number of Pets

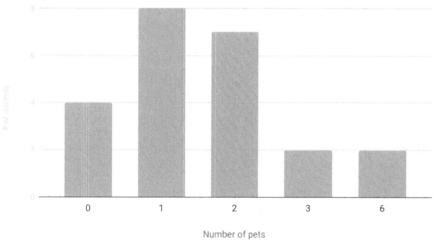

So, 4 people had 0 pets, 8 people had 1 pet, 7 people had 2 pets, and so on.

A stem and leaf plot breaks up the data into the 10s and 1s place of the data.

Test Scores

Stem	Leaf
7	4 6 7 7
8	2 3 8 9 9
9	3 4 4 5 8

So, the scores from the first row were 74, 76, 77, and 77

A scatter plot includes all of the data points with their x and y coordinates

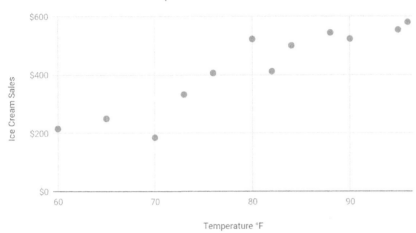

Ice Cream Sales vs. Temperature °F

So, when the temperature was 60°, they sold about $200 worth of ice cream.

The line of best fit is used to make a prediction or find an expected value from a scatter plot. This is the line that best fits between all of the data points.

Ice Cream Sales vs. Temperature °F

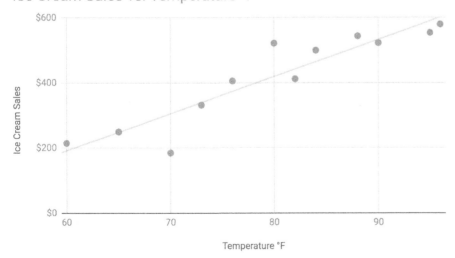

To make a prediction, do NOT use the points graphed. Instead, use the line of best fit.

Example:

The graph below shows an ice cream shop's sales with the temperature high recorded during that day of sales. How much ice cream would the shop expect to sell if the temperature were 70°?

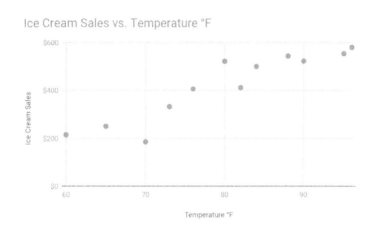

First, graph the line of best fit:

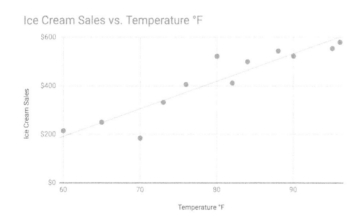

Next, use that line and NOT the data points to find the expected value.

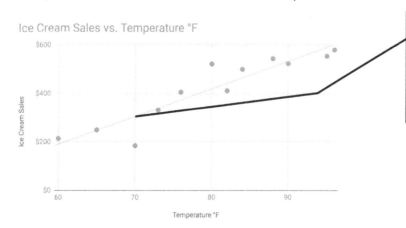

At 70° on the x axis, the value on the y axis is $300. So, the answer is $300

1. The following chart shows the number of hours students studied and their corresponding test scores.

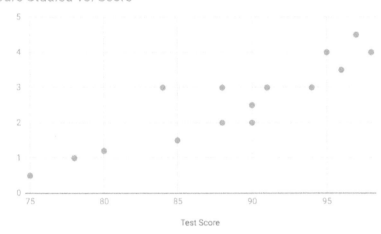

What score would a student who studied for 2 hours expect to earn?

(A) 80

(B) 85

(C) 88

(D) 90

2. The chart below shows the average number of miles players ran over spring break by sports teams. Which team had the lowest average?

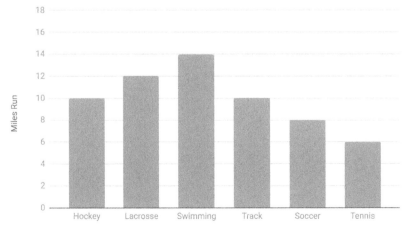

(A) Tennis

(B) Hockey

(C) Swimming

(D) Track

3. Alison surveyed her class and asked which they prefer: lions, tigers or bears. The pie chart below shows the results.

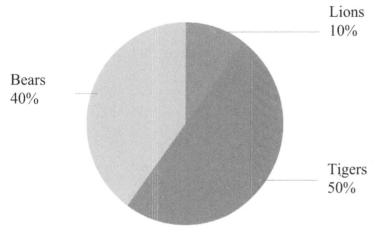

Which data corresponds to the sample?

(A) 15 prefer tigers, 10 prefer bears, 10 prefer lions

(B) 15 prefer tigers, 5 prefer bears, 1 prefers lions

(C) 15 prefer tigers, 8 prefer bears, 7 prefer lions

(D) 15 prefer tigers, 3 prefer lions, 12 prefer bears

4. The graph shows the water level in each of four different water tanks over an 8-hour period. Which water tank has the greatest hourly increase in water level?

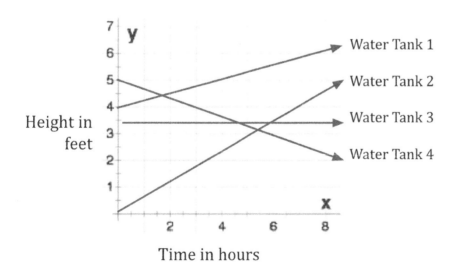

(A) Water tank 1

(B) Water tank 2

(C) Water tank 3

(D) Water tank 4

5. The following chart shows the number of birds spotted everyday by a birdwatcher. On which day were the highest number of birds spotted?

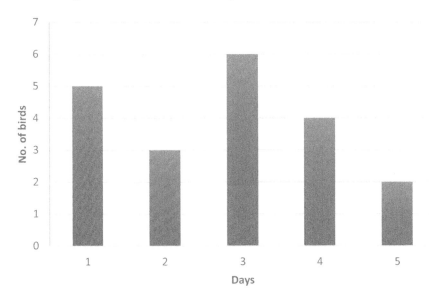

(A) 5

(B) 4

(C) 3

(D) 2

6. A farm has 3 crops which earn the farm a total of $60,000 every year. A pie-chart shows the share of the revenues (in %) of the 3 crops. How much revenue did the farm earn from selling tomatoes?

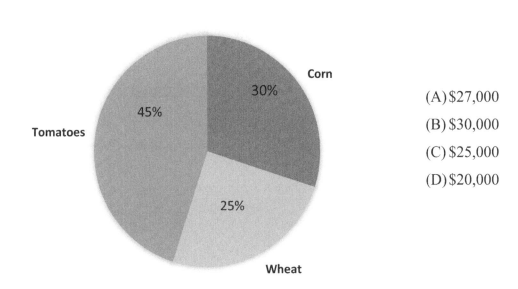

(A) $27,000

(B) $30,000

(C) $25,000

(D) $20,000

7. The bar graph shows the monthly sales of a novel. How many copies of the novel were sold in August?

Monthly Book Sales

(A) 35,000

(B) 28,000

(C) 30,000

(D) 32,000

8. To predict how two groups of people would vote on a proposal, samples of each group were surveyed to see if they would vote YES or NO on the proposal. The percent of each sample surveyed and the number of YES and NO responses are shown in the table.

Group	A	B
Percent of Group Surveyed	50%	20%
Number of YES votes	18	5
Number of NO votes	12	10

The results above can be used to predict how many people will vote for and against the proposal when all members of both groups vote.

Column A

The predicted number of NO votes when all members in Group A vote.

Column B

The predicted number of YES votes when all members in Group B vote.

(A) Column A is greater.

(B) Column B is greater.

(C) Column A and Column B are equal.

(D) The relationship cannot be determined from the information given.

9. Two car sellers deal in the same car model. The number of cars sold every month by them is shown below. Each car sold for $20,000.

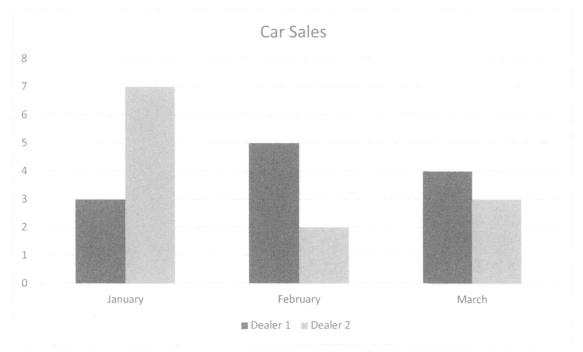

	Column A		Column B
	Sales by Dealer 1		Sales by Dealer 2

(A) Column A is greater

(B) Column B is greater

(C) Columns A and B are equal.

(D) The relationship cannot be determined from the information given.

10. 250 people out of 1000 voters, voted for party A in an election. If a pie chart of the results was created, what shape would be made by the vote share of party A?

(A) A semi-circle

(B) A full circle

(C) A quarter of a circle

(D) An eighth of a circle

1. **The correct answer is 'B'**

Remember to use the line of best fit. At 2 hours, the expected score from the line of best fit, would be 85.

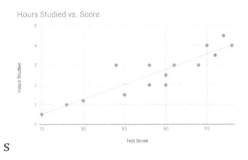

s

2. **The correct answer is 'A'**

The tennis team ran an average of 6 miles per player. The bar is also the lowest, so it had the lowest average.

3. **The correct answer is 'D'**

50% prefer tigers. Each data set option has 15 who prefer tigers, so the total must be 30.

These are the only two sets that add up to 30:

15 prefer tigers, 8 prefer bears, 7 prefer lions

15 prefer tigers, 12 prefer bears, 3 prefer lions

In the first data set more prefer bears than lions, but only 10% prefer lions and 40% prefer bears

So, **15 prefer tigers, 12 prefer bears, 3 prefer lions** is the only option.

4. **The correct answer is 'A'**

Water tank 1 goes up 1.5 ft every hour

Water tank 2 goes up .25 ft every hour

Water tank 3 goes down .5 ft every hour

Water tank 4 does not increase or decrease

Water tank 1 increases at the highest rate

5. **The correct answer is 'C'**

The highest number of birds (6) were spotted on day 3.

6. **The correct answer is 'A'**

Tomatoes contribute 45% to the total yearly sales of the farm. Also, the total yearly income of the farm is $60,000. So, tomatoes earn the farm $\frac{45}{100} \times 60{,}000 = \$27{,}000$

7. **The correct answer is 'C'**

The number of copies of the novel sold in August was 30,000.

8. **The correct answer is 'B'**

Column A

When 50% were surveyed, 12 would vote NO.

So, if 100% were surveyed, we would predict that **24** would vote NO.

Column B

When 20% were surveyed, 5 would vote Yes. 20% x 5 is 100%. So if 100% were surveyed **25** (5 x 5) would vote yes.

Column B is greater

9. **The correct answer is 'C'**

Though the sales of the two dealers vary from month to month, but they sell 12 cars each at the end of 3 months. So, they earn equal revenues.

10. **The correct answer is 'C'**

250 is a quarter of a 1000 and so the 250 voters of party A will represent a quarter of the pie-chart.

Mean, Median, Mode and Range

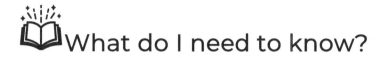 What do I need to know?

Mean (Average)	Add up all of the values and divide by the number of values
Median	Order the numbers and find the middle number
Mode	Find the data point that occurs the most times
Range	Subtract the lowest number from the highest number

 Example:

Find the mean, median, mode and range on the stem and leaf plot below.

Points in a Match

Stem	Leaf
1	2 3 4 4
2	1 3
3	0 3

Mean: *Add up all of the values and divide by the number of values*

12 + 13 + 14 + 14 + 21 + 23 + 30 + 33 = 160

There are 8 scores total, so we now divide 160 by 8.

160 ÷ 8 = 20

Mean = 20

Median: *Order the numbers and find the middle number.*

In a stem and leaf plot, the numbers are already ordered. So, cross off the lowest number then the highest one in pairs, until you find the middle number.

Stem	Leaf
1	2 3 4 4
2	1 3
3	0 3

→

Stem	Leaf
1	2 3 4 4
2	1 3
3	0 3

→

Stem	Leaf
1	2 3 4 4
2	1 3
3	0 3

The remaining numbers are 14 and 21. Because there are two numbers in the middle, we need to find the number directly between these two numbers. 17.5 is 3.5 above 14 and 3.5 below 21.

17.5 is the median.

Mode: *Find the data point that occurs the most times.*

3 occurs many times in the leaf column, but each time it has a different stem. The number that occurs most is 14.

Range: *Subtract the lowest number from the highest number.*

Stem	Leaf
1	2 3 4 4
2	1 3
3	0 3

Highest number: 33

Lowest number: 12

33 – 12 = 21

21 is the range.

1. The chart below shows the average number of miles players ran over spring break by sports teams.

Average Miles Run by Sports Teams

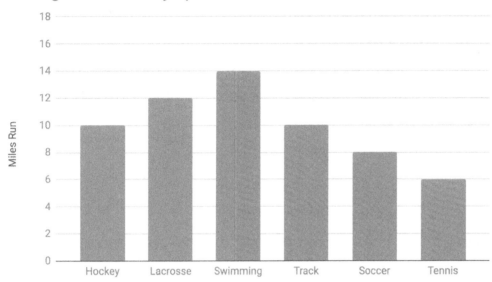

What is the mean distance run overall?

(A) 8

(B) 10

(C) 12

(D) 14

2. The stem and leaf plot below shows a series of temperatures recorded.

Stem	Leaf
6	4 5 7 8
7	5 6 7
8	4 5 8 9

What is the median?

    (A) 68

    (B) 75

    (C) 76

    (D) 77

3. The following chart shows the number of hours students studied and their corresponding test scores.

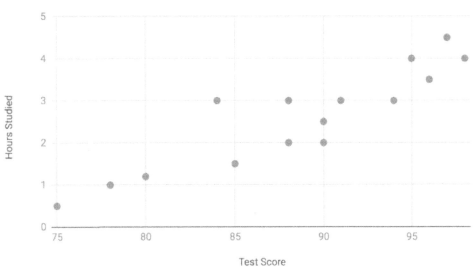

Hours Studied vs. Score

Column A	**Column B**
The range of the test scores	The median test score

(A) Column A is greater

(B) Column B is greater

(C) Column A and Column B are equal

(D) The relationship cannot be determined with the information given

4. Carlos played a game three times and had an average of 25 points per game. If he played one more time and scored 29 points, what would be his new average?

(A) 25

(B) 26

(C) 27

(D) 29

5. Kara surveyed her class to find out how many siblings each student had. The following chart shows the data.

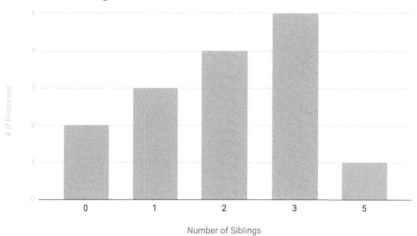

Number of Siblings

Column A

The mode of the data

Column B

The median of the data

(A) Column A is greater

(B) Column B is greater

(C) Column A and Column B are equal

(D) The relationship cannot be determined with the information given

6. The mean of 10 numbers is 55. What would be the new mean if 110 were added to the set of numbers?

(A) 56

(B) 60

(C) 61

(D) 66

7. A football team scores 3, 0, 1, 2 and 5 goals in 5 matches. What is the median of this data?

(A) 0

(B) 5

(C) 2

(D) 1

8. The weights of 5 dogs were observed and recorded as 30 kg, 25 kg, 27 kg, 30 kg and 32 kg. What is the range of this data?

    (A) 6 kg

    (B) 5 kg

    (C) 4 kg

    (D) 7 kg

9. The number of hours that a student studies for in a particular week are as follows:

    2, 3, 4, 2, 2, 5, 4. What is the mode of the data?

    (A) 2

    (B) 3

    (C) 4

    (D) 5

10. Four people work at a store. Their ages are 32, 28, 54 and 41 years. What is the mean of their ages?

    (A) 32

    (B) 36.5

    (C) 39

    (D) 41.5

1. The correct answer is 'B'

Mean = <u>Sum of the Data</u>

        # of Values

$10 + 12 + 14 + 10 + 8 + 6 = 60$

There were 6 values

$60/6 = 10$

10 is the mean

2. The correct answer is 'C'

The median is the middle number

Stem	Leaf
6	~~4~~5~~7~~~~8~~
7	5 6 ~~7~~
8	~~4~~~~5~~~~8~~~~9~~

3. The correct answer is 'B'

<u>Column A</u>

Maximum: 98

Minimum: 75

Range 23

<u>Column B</u>

The Median will be the middle score. No score is even close to 23, so we know the median will be much higher than the range. The median is 90. Column B is greater.

4. The correct answer is 'B'

$25 + 25 + 25 =$ Total points for the first 3 games = 75

$75 + 29$ (new score) = 104 (New total)

$104/4 = 26$

New Mean = 26

5. **The correct answer is 'A'**

   Column A

   The mode of the data.

   5 people have 3 siblings, so 3 is the response that occurs the most.

   Mode: 3

   Column B

   Median: 2

6. **The correct answer is 'B'**

   The mean of the first 10 numbers is 55. So, their sum is 55×10=550. Add the new number, 110 to 550. 110+550=660. 660 ÷ 11 = 60.

7. **The correct answer is 'C'**

   After arranging the data in ascending order we get 0,1,2,3,5. Since, there are odd number of data points, the median is the number in the middle of all of them. So, here the median is 2.

8. **The correct answer is 'D'**

   The highest observed value is 32 and the lowest observed value is 25. So, the range of the data is 32-25=7.

9. **The correct answer is 'A'**

   2 appears the most number of times in the data set.

10. **The correct answer is 'C'**

    Mean= Sum of the values/ number of values

    Mean = (32+28+54+42)/4=39.

New Mean

Common tricky question types

These problems ask you to find the value that would need to be added to a data set to make a new mean.

What do I need to know?

To find a **new mean**:

Original sum + New number = Desired Sum.

Original sum: the mean x the number of values (the sum of all of the original values)

Desired sum: the new mean that is desired x the new number of values

Example:

The average of 5 numbers is 90. What number needs to be added to the set to make the new mean 95?

Original sum + New number = Desired Sum.

Original sum: 5 x 90 (number of values x original mean) = 450

Desired sum: 6 x 95 (the new number of values x new mean) = 570

450 + new number = 570

450 + **120** = 570

So, 120 is the new number.

1. A set of 4 numbers has a mean of 22. What additional number should be added to the set to make the mean 25?

   (A) 25

   (B) 30

   (C) 35

   (D) 37

2. Mari was playing a game where the goal was to score as many points as possible. After 6 rounds, her average score was 11. What would she need to score on the 7th round to raise her average score to 12?

   (A) 12

   (B) 16

   (C) 18

   (D) 20

3. Marshall walked an average of 5 miles a day for 10 days for his school walking competition. He has 2 more days to walk. How many miles should he walk each day for the next two days to raise his average to 6 miles a day? (He wants to divide his miles evenly over the next 2 days)

   (A) 6

   (B) 8

   (C) 10

   (D) 11

4. Marian ate an average of 10 blueberries a day for 7 days. She wanted to lower her average to 9 a day. How many blueberries should she eat on the 8th day to lower her average to 9 per day?

   (A) 0

   (B) 2

   (C) 4

   (D) 9

5. Masie earned an average of 85% on her first four math tests. Her teacher decided to count her test twice. What is the lowest score she could score to keep her average at 80% or above?

   (A) 65

   (B) 70

   (C) 75

   (D) 80

6. In a singing competition a singer needs at least 8.5 points to qualify for the next round. Three judges give her 10, 7 and 7 points. What is the minimum score that the fourth judge must give her so that she may qualify for the next round?

   (A) 9

   (B) 10

   (C) 8

   (D) 7

7. Myra earned an average of 100 points in each of 9 rounds of her video game. In the next round, she scored 0 points. What was her new average?

(A) 80 points

(B) 90 points

(C) 95 points

(D) 100 points

8. A dog needed to eat an average of 3 cups of dog food per day. If the dog ate 8 cups over the first 3 days, how many more cups would the dog need to eat on the 4th day to make the average 3 cups per day?

(A) 3 cups

(B) 3.5 cups

(C) 4 cups

(D) 4.5 cups

9. A penguin eats 10 fishes a day on average for 3 days. If it eats 6 fishes on the 4th day what is the new mean of the number of fishes eaten?

(A) 7

(B) 8

(C) 9

(D) 6

10. A tourist attraction has 2000 visitors on average for 6 days of a week. How many days would need to visit on the 7th day to raise the daily average by 100 for the week?

(A) 2000 visitors

(B) 2100 visitors

(C) 2600 visitors

(D) 2700 visitors

1. **The correct answer is 'D'**

   The original sum of the numbers is 88.

   With 5 numbers, the new sum needs to be

   25 x 5 or 125.

   88 + x = 125

   x = 37

2. **The correct answer is 'C'**

   Original Sum= Mean x # of values

   Original Sum= 6 x 11 = 66

   New Sum = New Mean x New # of Values

   New Sum = 7 x 12 = 84

   66 + ___ = 84

   84 - 66 = 18

3. **The correct answer is 'D'**

   Original Sum= Original Mean x Number of

   Values

   Original Sum = 5 x 10 = 50

   New Sum = New Mean x Number of

   Values

   New Sum = 6 x 12 = 72

   Original Sum + ___ + ___ =New Sum

   50 + ___ + ___ = 72

   -50   -50

   ___ + ___ = 22

   11 + 11 = 22

   11 per day

4. **The correct answer is 'B'**

   Original Sum = Original mean + Number

   of values

   Original Sum = 10 x 7 = 70

   New Sum = New Mean + Number of

   Values

   New Sum = 9 x 8 = 72

   Original Sum + ___ = New Sum

   70 + ___ = 72

   ___ = 2

   She should eat 2

5. **The correct answer is 'B'**

   Original Sum = 85 x 4 = 340

   New Sum = 80 x 6 = 480 (New average

   because the lowest average she wants is

   80)

   Original + ___ + ___ = New

   340 + ___ + ___ = 480

   -340   -340

   ___ + ___ = 140

   70 + 70 = 140

   Lowest score is 70

6. **The correct answer is 'B'**

   Original Sum = 10 + 7 + 7 =24

   New Sum = 8.5 x 4 = 34

   24 + ___ = 34

   She must score a 10.

7. The correct answer is 'B'

Original Sum = 100 x 9 = 900

New Sum = 900

New Average = New Sum/10

90

8. The correct answer is 'C'

Original Sum = 8 cups

New Sum = 3 cups x 4 days

Original + ___ = New

8 + ___ = 12

___ = 4

4 cups

9. The correct answer is 'C'

Original Sum = 10 x 3 = 30

New Sum = 30+ 6 = 36

36 fish ÷ 4 days = 9 fish

10. The correct answer is 'D'

Original Sum = 2000 x 6 = 12,000

New Sum = 2100 x 7 = 14,700

Original + ___ = New

12,000 + ____ = 14,700

___ = 2,700 visitors

Probability and Combinations

 What do I need to know?

Probability	<u># of desired outcomes</u> # of possible outcomes	The probability of rolling a 2 on a 6-sided die is $\frac{1}{6}$ because there is 1 side with a 2 on it and there are 6 possible outcomes on the die.
AND problems	Probability of the first event x the probability of the second event	The probability of rolling a 2 **and** then another 2 is $$\frac{1}{6} \times \frac{1}{6} = \frac{1}{36}$$
OR problems	Probability of the first event + the probability of the second event.	The probability of rolling a 2 **or** a 4 is $$\frac{1}{6} + \frac{1}{6} = \frac{2}{6} \rightarrow \frac{1}{3}$$
Combinations	Multiply the number of options for each category	There are 2 drinks, 3 sides, and 4 sandwiches. How many combinations of meals can be made with one drink, one side, and one sandwich? 2 x 3 x 4 = 24
Complementary Events	One event and the opposite event. The probability will add up to 1.	The probability of rolling an odd number and the probability of rolling an even number.

Example:

A bag has 5 blue marbles, 3 yellow marbles, and 2 red marbles. What is the probability of choosing a blue marble, replacing it, and then choosing a yellow marble?

Probability of choosing a blue marble = $\frac{5\ blue\ marbles}{10\ total\ marbles} = \frac{5}{10}\ or\ \frac{1}{2}$

Probability of choosing a yellow marble = $\frac{3\ yellow\ marbles}{10\ total\ marbles} = \frac{3}{10}$

We are looking for the probability of choosing a blue marble AND a yellow marble, so we multiply!

$$\frac{1}{2} \times \frac{3}{10} = \frac{3}{20}$$

3/20 is the final answer.

How do I remember?

Just remember that AND = x and OR = +.

1. A bag contains 4 red marbles, 3 green marbles, and 2 blue marbles.

Column A	Column B
The probability of choosing a red marble	The probability of choosing a green or a blue marble

(A) Column A is greater

(B) Column B is greater

(C) Column A and Column B are equal

(D) The relationship cannot be determined with the information given

2. On a regular sided die, what is the probability of rolling an odd number and then an even number?

(A) 1/6

(B) 1/4

(C) 1/2

(D) 1

3. An ice cream shop has 6 flavors, 5 toppings, and 2 syrups. The shop randomly gives its customers a scoop of ice cream, one topping, and one syrup. What is the probability that Sheila will get her 1 favorite flavor, 1 favorite topping, and 1 favorite syrup?

(A) 1/60

(B) 1/30

(C) 1/10

(D) 3/13

4. A restaurant has 6 entrees, 4 sides, and 5 types of drinks. A meal combo includes one entree, one side, and one type of drink. How many combinations could be created for the meal combo?

(A) 15

(B) 30

(C) 60

(D) 120

5. Darts are thrown at random at the dartboard. What is the probability that it will land in the shaded region?

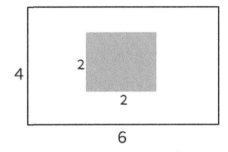

(A) 1/2

(B) 1/6

(C) 1/4

(D) 1/3

(E)

6. A bag contains 6 red marbles, 4 green marbles, and 2 blue marbles.

Column A	Column B
The probability of choosing a red	The probability of choosing a green or blue marble

(A) Column A is greater

(B) Column B is greater

(C) Column A and Column B are equal

(D) The relationship cannot be determined with the information given

7. On a regular sided die, what is the probability of rolling a 4 and then a 6 if you roll it twice?

(A) 1/36

(B) 1/12

(C) 1/6

(D) 1/3

8. An ice cream shop has 4 flavors, 5 toppings, and 2 syrups. The shop randomly gives its customers a scoop of ice cream, one topping, and one syrup. What is the probability that Sheila will get her 1 favorite flavor, 1 favorite topping, and 1 favorite syrup?

(A) 1/60

(B) 1/40

(C) 1/30

(D) 3/11

9. A restaurant has 10 entrees, 4 sides, and 4 types of drinks. A meal combo includes one entree, one side, and one type of drink. How many combinations could be created for the meal combo?

(A) 18

(B) 60

(C) 120

(D) 160

10. Darts are thrown at random at the dartboard. What is the probability that it will land in the shaded region?

(A) 1/5

(B) 2/5

(C) 3/5

(D) 4/5

1. The correct answer is 'B'

Column A

$$\frac{4 \text{ red marbles}}{9 \text{ marbles total}} \rightarrow \frac{4}{9}$$

Column B

$$\frac{3 \text{ green}+2 \text{ blue marbles}}{9 \text{ marbles total}} \rightarrow \frac{5}{9}$$

2. The correct answer is 'B'

And = x

Probability of rolling an odd number

3/6 --> 1/2

Probability of rolling an even number

3/6 --> 1/2

Probability of rolling an odd number AND

Probability of rolling an even number

1/2 x 1/2

¼

3. The correct answer is 'A'

Probability of favorite flavor: 1/6

Probability of favorite topping: 1/5

Probability of favorite syrup: 1/2

Flavor, topping AND syrup--> Multiply

1/6 x 1/5 x ½

1/60

4. The correct answer is 'D'

For combinations, you multiply all of the options.

6 entrees x 4 sides x 5 drinks

120

5. The correct answer is 'B'

$$\frac{Area\ of\ the\ shaded\ region}{Area\ of\ the\ whole}$$

Area of the shaded region: $2 \times 2 = 4$

Area of the whole: $4 \times 6 = 24$

$$\frac{4}{24} = \frac{1}{6}$$

6. The correct answer is 'C'

Column A

$$\frac{6 \text{ red marbles}}{12 \text{ marbles total}} \rightarrow \frac{6}{12} \rightarrow \frac{1}{2}$$

Column B

$$\frac{4 \text{ green}+2 \text{ blue marbles}}{12 \text{ marbles total}} \rightarrow \frac{6}{12} \rightarrow \frac{1}{2}$$

Columns A and B are equal.

7. **The correct answer is 'A'**

And = ×

Probability of rolling a 4 is 1/6

Probability of rolling a 6 is 1/6

Probability of rolling a 4 AND Probability of rolling a 6

$1/6 \times 1/6$

$1/36$

8. **The correct answer is 'B'**

Probability of favorite flavor: 1/4

Probability of favorite topping: 1/5

Probability of favorite syrup: 1/2

Flavor, topping AND syrup--> Multiply

1/4 x 1/5 x 1/2

1/40

9. **The correct answer is 'D'**

For combinations, you multiply all of the options.

10 entrees x 4 sides x 4 drinks

160

10. **The correct answer is 'B'**

Shaded region: 3 x 10 = 30

30 x 2 = 60

Whole: 10 x 15 = 150

$$\frac{\text{Area of the Shaded Region}}{\text{Area of the Whole}} = \frac{60}{150} = \frac{6}{15} = \frac{2}{5}$$

Data and Probability Review

1. A bag contains 3 red marbles, 5 green marbles and 4 blue marbles. You draw one marble, put it back, and draw another. What is the probability of choosing a red marble and a blue marble?
   (A) 1/12
   (B) 3/12
   (C) 5/12
   (D) 7/12

2. A bag contains 3 red marbles, 5 green marbles and 4 blue marbles. You draw one marble. What is the probability of choosing a red marble or a green marble?
   (A) 1/12
   (B) 5/12
   (C) 1/3
   (D) 2/3

3. An ice cream shop has 7 flavors, 3 toppings, and 2 syrups. If each sundae has one flavor, one topping, and one syrup, how many possible combinations are there?
   (A) 12
   (B) 21
   (C) 38
   (D) 42

4. A stack of cards has cards numbered 1-9. Which of the following would describe complementary events?
   (A) Choosing an odd number and then choosing an even number
   (B) Choosing a 5 and then choosing another 5
   (C) Choosing a number below 4 and then choosing an even number
   (D) Choosing an even number and then choosing another even number

5. You roll a standard die with 6 sides

Column A	Column B
The probability of rolling an even number	The probability of rolling an odd number

   (A) Column A is greater
   (B) Column B is greater
   (C) Column A and Column B are equal
   (D) The relationship cannot be determined with the information given

6. A set of numbers has a mean of 50. The highest number is 56 and the range is 9. What is the lowest number?

(A) 45

(B) 46

(C) 47

(D) 48

7. A set of 4 numbers has a mean of 12. What number would need to be added to the set to make the mean 11?

(A) -1

(B) 5

(C) 7

(D) 11

8. What is the mode of the set of numbers in this stem and leaf plot?

Stem	Leaf
1	2 3 4 4
2	3 4 6 6 6 7 7
3	4 5 7 8

(A) 4

(B) 6

(C) 26

(D) 27

9. What is the range of the set of numbers in this stem and leaf plot?

Stem	Leaf
1	2 3 4 4
2	3 4 6 6 6 7 7
3	4 5 7 8

(A) 12

(B) 24

(C) 26

(D) 38

10. Sam sells each of his toys for the same price. Each order includes a standard shipping fee regardless of how many toys are ordered. What is the shipping fee?

Number of Toys	Cost of the Order
1	$9
2	$14
3	$19
4	$24

(A) $3

(B) $4

(C) $5

(D) $6

Use the following chart for **questions 10 and 11**. The chart below shows the number of hours a person studied compared to their score on a test.

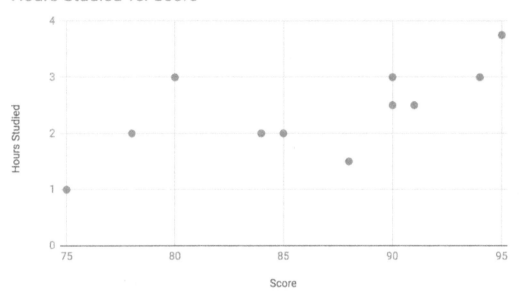

11. Using the chart above, what was the median score?

(A) 85

(B) 88

(C) 90

(D) 95

12. Using the chart above, what was the average number of hours the person studied?

(A) 2

(B) $2\frac{4}{11}$

(C) $2\frac{7}{11}$

(D) 3

13. Students were asked if they prefer dogs, cats or birds.

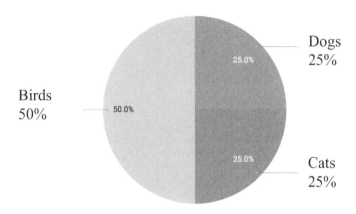

Which of the following data sets could correspond with this chart?

(A) 8 prefer birds, 5 prefer dogs, 3 prefer cats

(B) 8 prefer birds, 4 prefer dogs, 4 prefer cats

(C) 8 prefer birds, 6 prefer dogs, 6 prefer cats

(D) 8 prefer birds, 4 prefer dogs, 6 prefer cats

14. A student surveyed her class about how many siblings each person has.

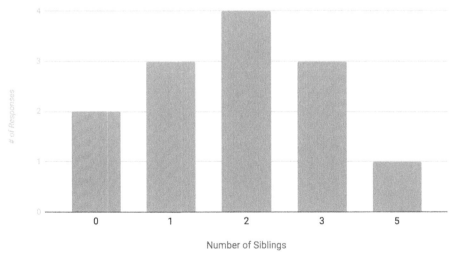

What is the mode number of siblings?

(A) 1

(B) 2

(C) 3

(D) 4

Use the chart below to answer question 15.

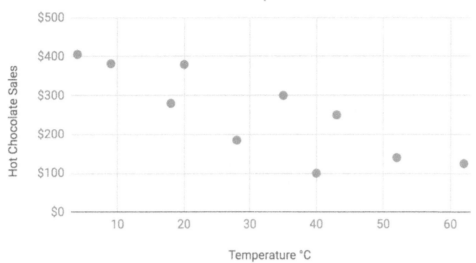

15. What would be the expected hot chocolate sales if the temperature were 40 degrees?

    (A) $100

    (B) $180

    (C) $240

    (D) $300

1. **The correct answer is 'A'**

   A bag contains 3 red marbles, 5 green marbles and 4 blue marbles. You draw one marble, put it back, and draw another. What is the probability of choosing a red marble and a blue marble?

   and = x

   Probability of choosing a red marble=

   3/ 12 or 1/4

   Probability of choosing a blue marble=

   4/ 12 or 1/3

   1/3 x 1/4 = 1/12

2. **The correct answer is 'D'**

   Or = +

   Probability of choosing a green marble:

   3/12

   Probability of choosing a green marble:

   5/12

   3/12 + 5/12 = 8/12 → 2/3

3. **The correct answer is 'D'**

   7 flavors x 3 toppings x 2 syrups

   7 x 3 x 2

   21 x 2

   42

4. **The correct answer is 'A'**

   Complementary events are two opposite events whose probabilities add up to 1

5. **The correct answer is 'C'**

   Column A

   Even number

   2, 4, 6

   SO → 3/6

   Column B

   Odd number

   1, 3, 5

   SO → 3/6

   Columns A and B are equal

6. **The correct answer is "C"**

   The mean is irrelevant here.

   Highest number: 56

   Range: 9

   56-9 = 47

   Lowest number: 47

7. **The correct answer is "C"**

   Old Sum:

   # of value x mean

   4 numbers x 12

   4 x 12= 48

   New Sum

   # of value x desired mean

   5 numbers x 11

   55

   48 + ? = 55

   48 + 7 = 55

   New number is 7

8. The correct answer is "C"

Pay attention to both the stem and the leaf. 26 occurs 3 times so 26 is the mode. While other numbers in the ones digit column occur more than 3 times, they do not occur more than 3 times with the same number in the tens column. For example, the numbers with 4 as a leaf are 14, 14, 24, and 34.

9. The correct answer is "C"

Highest number: 38

Lowest number: 12

Range: 26

10. The correct answer is "B"

The cost goes up 5 dollars each time, so the cost of each toy is 5 dollars.

The shipping fee is 4 dollars because 1 toy costs 5 dollars + the shipping fee. The cost of the order for 1 toy is $9. So, the shipping fee is 4.

11. The correct answer is "B"

Cross out the numbers on the chart. Cancel out the lowest number and the high number at the same time. Then repeat with the next lowest and the next highest. The middle number is 88.

12. The correct answer is "B"

Write down each data point for how many hours an individual studied regardless of their score:

1, 2, 3, 2, 2, 1.5, 2.5, 2.5, 3, 3, 3.5

Average = $\frac{\underline{\text{sum of the numbers}}}{\text{number of values}}$

$$\frac{1+2+3+2+2+1.5+2.5+2.5+3+3+3.5}{11}$$

$$= \frac{26}{11} = 2\frac{4}{11}$$

13. The correct answer is "B"

Half prefer birds, so if 8 prefer birds, there must be 16 total.

The number who prefer dogs and cats must be equal, so these must be 4 each.

14. The correct answer is "B"

The highest bar (so the one with the most frequency) corresponds with 2 siblings, so that is the mode.

15. The correct answer is "B"

Remember to use the line of best fit!

Full Test Sections

Full Quantitative Reasoning Section

37 Questions – 35 Minutes

Part One – Word Problems

1. The graph below shows the number of hours each month Darshan practiced the violin. What is the average number of hours he practiced each month?

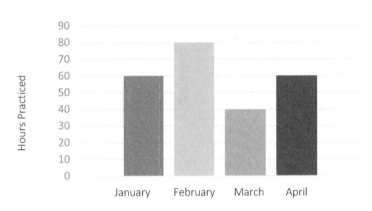

   (A) 70

   (B) 65

   (C) 60

   (D) 75

2. What is the area of a trapezoid with parallel base lengths 3 cm and 5 cm and a height of 2 cm?

   (A) 8 cm²

   (B) 10 cm²

   (C) 6 cm²

   (D) 9 cm²

3. Which number is closest to the square root of 104?

   (A) 9

   (B) 10

   (C) 11

   (D) 12

4. A giant cube shaped statue is going to be installed in the park. The volume of the cube is 125 m². What is the length of one of the sides o: the cube?

   (A) 4 m

   (B) 5 m

   (C) 6 m

   (D) 7 m

5. If $4x + 2 = 10$, what is the value of $2x + 1$?

   (A) 2

   (B) 3

   (C) 5

   (D) 6

6. Two coins are tossed simultaneously. What is the probability that both coins land on heads?

   (A) ¼
   (B) ½
   (C) 1
   (D) 2

7. 93% of the students in Sarah's class are wearing sneakers today. Sarah has 200 people in her class. How many people are wearing sneakers?

   (A) 93
   (B) 166
   (C) 186
   (D) 193

8. A set of 4 numbers has a mean of 8. What number needs to be added to the set to create a mean that is 2 more than the original mean?

   (A) 8
   (B) 10
   (C) 16
   (D) 18

9. Jerry had 48 math problems for homework this week. Today, he completed the first 25%. How many problems did he finish?

   (A) 10
   (B) 12
   (C) 24
   (D) 25

10. A bag contains 4 yellow candies, 1 blue candies, 6 red candies, and 1 green candy. Star selects one candy, replaces it, then selects another. What is the probability that she chose a yellow candy and then a red candy?

    (A) $\frac{1}{144}$

    (B) $\frac{1}{12}$

    (C) $\frac{1}{6}$

    (D) $\frac{5}{6}$

11. A large cube was built using small cubes with a side length of 1. The large cube has a side length of 4. How many small cubes were used to build the large cube?

    (A) 4
    (B) 16
    (C) 24
    (D) 64

12. There are 20 pizzas for an upcoming party. 1/4 of the pizzas are topped with pepperoni, 2/5 topped with veggies, and the rest are cheese. How many pizzas are cheese?

    (A) 6
    (B) 7
    (C) 8
    (D) 10

13. For any number ⊕g, ⊕g = 4g – 6. What is the value of ⊕ 5?

      (A) 14

      (B) 16

      (C) 20

      (D) 26

14. A teacher gave a quiz with 5 questions. She awarded points according to the table below. Which equation best represents the way she awarded points?

Correct Answers (C)	Points (P)
1	22
2	42
3	62
4	82
5	102

      (A) $P = 20C + 2$

      (B) $P = 20 + 2C$

      (C) $P = 100 - 20C$

      (D) $P = 10C + 12$

15. Which is a possible net for this cube?

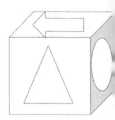

(A)

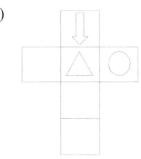

(B)

(C)

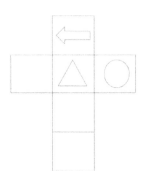

(D)

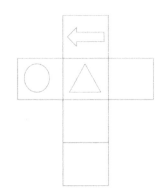

16. An ice cream stand recorded its sales based on the outside temperature. The data is recorded in the table below.

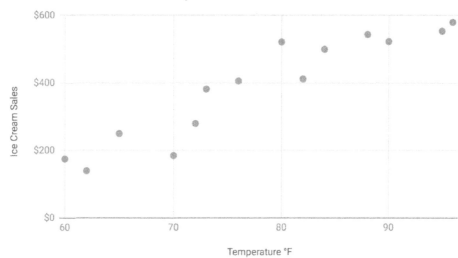

If the outside temperature were 80°, how much money would the ice cream stand expect to make?

(A) $350

(B) $400

(C) $500

(D) $550

17. Molly is 3 times as old as Tanya. Tanya is 4 years younger than Grant. If Grant is 13, how old is Molly?

(A) 3

(B) 9

(C) 18

(D) 27

18. If 3/4 of a pool can be filled in one hour, how many minutes will it take to fill the rest of the pool?

(A) 15

(B) 20

(C) 30

(D) 40

19. Which expression has the greatest value?

(A) 30% of 2000

(B) 0.31 of 2000

(C) 1/4 of 2000

(D) 1/3 of 2000

20. How many fourths are in 3 ¼ ?

(A) 1

(B) 4

(C) 12

(D) 13

Part Two – Quantitative Comparisons

Directions: Compare the quantity in Column A and Column B. All questions in Part Two have these answer choices:

(A) The quantity in Column A is greater.

(B) The quantity in Column B is greater.

(C) The two quantities are equal.

(D) The relationship cannot be determined from the information given.

---

21. $y = 2x + 1$

Column A	Column B
The slope of the line.	The value of y when x = 0.

22.

Column A	Column B
The hypotenuse of a right-angled triangle with base 4 and height 3.	6

23. A camera costs $150.

Column A	Column B
The cost after a 30% discount.	$120

24. The following data set is of the number of hours that a student studies for over the course of a week:

2, 3, 2, 2, 5, 4, 1

Column A	Column B
The average number of hours she studies over the whole month.	The mode of the data set.

25. A car crosses two stretches of a highway. One stretch is 30 miles long and the speed limit is 60 miles per hour. Another stretch is 40 miles long and the speed limit is 40 miles an hour. The driver is in a hurry but also adheres to the speed limits and so moves at the maximum speed limit.

Column A	Column B
Time taken to cover the entire stretch of 70 miles.	2 hours

26.

Column A	Column B
-5^2	$(-5)^2$

27.

Column A	Column B
The diameter of a circle with a circumference 16π.	The area of a square with a side length of 4.

28. | Column A | Column B |
| --- | --- |
| The probability of rolling a 2 or 3 on a 6 sided die. | 0.2 |

---

29. A class has 22 girls and 24 boys. 3 girls and 1 boy join the class in the new academic year.

Column A	Column B
% of girls in the class	% of boys in the class

---

30. Rhonda pours a full glass of juice for her friend. The friend then empties half the glass into a jar. The friend then drinks half of what is left in the glass.

Column A	Column B
Fraction of glass filled with juice	1/5

31. Lee scored the following number of points on after playing 6 rounds of a game 8, 9, 12, 3, 4, 6.

Column A	Column B
The mean of his scores.	The range of his scores

---

32. Cards numbered from 1 to 10 are well shuffled and a card is picked at random.

Column A	Column B
The probability of picking a card that is a multiple of 3.	1/2

---

33. $4x - 3 = x$

Column A	Column B
The value of x	The value of x^2

34.

Column A	Column B
The perimeter of this shape.	The perimeter of this shape.

 5, 6

 5, 3, 6

36.

Column A	Column B
$\sqrt{25 \times 4}$	$\sqrt{25} \times \sqrt{4}$

37. Diyandra received $1.35 in quarters, dimes, and nickels only. (Note: 1 quarter = $0.25; 1 dime = $.10; 1 nickel = $0.5)

Column A	Column B
The smallest number of coins Diyandra could have received	7

35. An item costs $500.

Column A	Column B
The amount saved after a 30% discount.	The amount saved after two 15% discounts.

Quantitative Reasoning Section – Answers

1. C
2. A
3. B
4. B
5. C
6. A
7. C
8. D
9. B
10. C
11. D
12. B
13. A
14. A

15. C
16. B
17. D
18. B
19. D
20. D
21. A
22. B
23. B
24. D
25. B
26. B
27. C
28. A

29. C
30. A
31. B
32. B
33. C
34. C
35. A
36. C
37. B

Scoring your Quantitative Reasoning Section

Use this chart to approximate your percentile score based on your number of correct answers.

Applying to 7th Grade:

Correct Answers	16-17	21-22	26-27
Percentile	25th	50th	75th

Applying to 8th Grade:

Correct Answers	17-18	22-23	29-30
Percentile	25th	50th	75th

A general rule of thumb to calculate your approximate stanine score is to take your # of correct answers and divide by 47. The number in the 10s digit of your percentage score is your approximate stanine score. This isn't a perfect rule, but it can be pretty accurate for the math sections

Percentile ——Stanine

1-3 —— 1

4-10——2

11-22——3

23-39——4

40-59——5

60-76——6

77-88——7

89-95——8

96-99——9

Full Mathematics Achievement Section

47 Questions – 40 Minutes

1. Which number has no positive factors except itself and 1?

   (A) 14

   (B) 21

   (C) 23

   (D) 27

2. Which expression is equal to 15?

   (A) 4 x (5 + 3) – 8

   (B) (4 x 5) + 3 – 8

   (C) 4 x (5 + 3 - 8)

   (D) 4 x 5 + 8 – 3

3. If 4& = 2@ and one @ is 14. What is the value of &?

   (A) 4

   (B) 7

   (C) 12

   (D) 14

4. If G = 3 (2x + y), what is G when x is 4 and y is 7?

   (A) 31

   (B) 33

   (C) 45

   (D) 47

5. Marsha and Fred kept track of their total sales for 4 weeks in the table below.

Week	Marsha's Total	Fred's Total
1	105.10	122.15
2	146.20	137.15
3	187.30	152.15
4	228.40	172.15

   After week 1, how much did Marsha sell each week?

   (A) $15

   (B) $31.10

   (C) $40.90

   (D) $41.10

6. Marcy scored an average of 14 points in each of the 6 rounds of a game. If her highest score was 17 and the range of her scores was 9, what was her lowest score?

   (A) 7

   (B) 8

   (C) 9

   (D) 10

7. A drawer contains 5 pairs of green socks, 8 pairs of blue socks, and 1 pair of white socks. A pair of socks is selected at random and replaced before a second pair is selected. Based on this scenario, which sentence describes complementary events?

(A) The first pair of socks is green and the second pair is blue or green

(B) The first pair of socks is blue and the second pair is green

(C) The first pair of socks is white and the second pair is blue or green

(D) The first pair of socks is blue or green and the second pair is blue or green

8. What is the sum of 6,889 + 8,778?

(A) 15,567

(B) 15,667

(C) 15,557

(D) 16,667

9. These two rectangles are similar. What is the value of x?

(A) 14

(B) 15

(C) 18

(D) 20

10. A student recorded her scores each month throughout the year. What was the range of her scores?

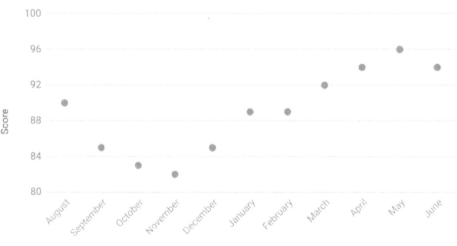

(A) 12

(B) 14

(C) 18

(D) 82

11. Which is equivalent to the expression:

$$\frac{40(66 + 34)}{5}$$

(A) 700

(B) 800

(C) 900

(D) 4,000

12. Today, Mariah's dance practice was two and a half times as long as it was yesterday. By what percent did her practice time increase?

(A) 25%

(B) 50%

(C) 150%

(D) 250%

13. There are 6 more fish than turtles in the pond. If there are 3 turtles in the pond, what fraction of the animals in the pond are turtles?

(A) 1/6

(B) 1/4

(C) 1/3

(D) 1/2

14. The number of calories, y, an adult can burn by swimming depends on the number of minutes, x, spent swimming according to the formula y = 7.5x + 1.5. What is the meaning of 7.5 in the formula?

(A) For every 1.5 minutes spent swimming, 7.5 calories are burned

(B) For every 7.5 minutes swimming, 1.5 calories are burned

(C) When 0 minutes are spent swimming, 7.5 calories are burned

(D) For every 1 minute spent swimming, 7.5 calories are burned

15. On a map, 6 centimeters equals 100 kilometers. If two cities are 21 centimeters apart, what is their actual distance apart?

(A) 300

(B) 350

(C) 600

(D) 650

16. In the equation a - 5 = - 3 - b, what is the value of (a + b)?

(A) -8

(B) -3

(C) 2

(D) 5

17. What is the value of g in the equation: $2\frac{1}{3} \div 1\frac{5}{6} = g$

(A) $1\frac{3}{11}$

(B) $1\frac{5}{11}$

(C) $2\frac{2}{5}$

(D) $2\frac{3}{5}$

18. In the following equation, what is the value of H: $\frac{H}{32} = \frac{15}{24}$

(A) 16

(B) 18

(C) 20

(D) 24

19. Of the 30% of the class that has a cat, 2/3 also have a hamster. What fraction of the class has a cat and a hamster?

(A) $\frac{1}{10}$

(B) $\frac{1}{6}$

(C) $\frac{1}{5}$

(D) $\frac{1}{4}$

20. Darren has 3 pairs of shoes, 4 pairs of pants, and 4 shirts. He has 1 favorite pairs of shoes, 1 favorite pair of pants, and 1 favorite shirt. If he randomly selects an outfit to wear, what is the probability that it will be one of his favorite pairs of shoes, his favorite pair of pants, or his favorite shirt?

(A) 1/48

(B) 1/24

(C) 1/12

(D) 2/11

21. What is the slope of the line:

$3x - 5y = -12$

(A) $-\frac{3}{5}$

(B) $\frac{3}{5}$

(C) 3

(D) -5

22. What type of quadrilateral is ABCD?

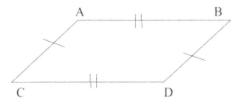

(A) Rhombus

(B) Trapezoid

(C) Parallelogram

(D) Rectangle

23. Gemma conducted a survey to find out if her classmates preferred apples, pears, or oranges. Which data corresponds to the sample of her classmates?

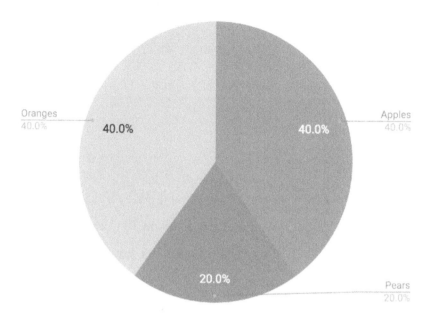

(A) 6 prefer apples, 6 prefer oranges, and 6 prefer pears

(B) 6 prefer apples, 6 prefer oranges, and 3 prefer pears

(C) 6 prefer apples, 3 prefer oranges, and 3 prefer pears

(D) 6 prefer apples, 5 prefer oranges, and 2 prefer pears

24. What is the value of the expression

3.24 x 1.6?

(A) 0.5184

(B) 5.184

(C) 51.84

(D) 518.4

25. Which is equivalent to the equation:

$$y = \frac{x}{3} + 4$$

(A) $3y + 4 = x$

(B) $3(x+y) = 4$

(C) $\frac{1}{3}x = y - 4$

(D) $y + 4 = \frac{1}{3}x$

26. Triangles ABC and triangles DEF are similar.

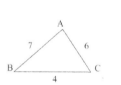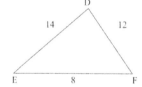

What is the ratio of triangle ABC to triangle DEF?

(A) 1 to 2

(B) 2 to 1

(C) 1 to 3

(D) 3 to 1

27. What type of transformation was performed?

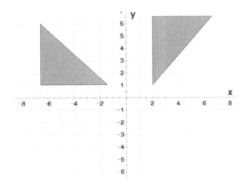

(A) Slide

(B) Reflection

(C) Rotation

(D) Shift

28. A band is putting on a concert. Profit is revenue minus cost. The concert will cost between 1,500 and 2,000 dollars. The concert will run for 3 nights with an expected audience of 400 people per night. If the tickets cost $10 each, approximately, what is the expected profit for this production?

(A) 6,000

(B) 8,000

(C) 10,000

(D) 14,000

29. What is the value of the expression

$1/4 + 1.78 + 2/5 + 1.6$?

(A) 3.78

(B) 3.83

(C) 4.03

(D) 4.13

30. Jamie can paint 4 boxes in 15 minutes. Mabel can paint 6 boxes in 30 minutes. If they both paint for 60 minutes, how many boxes will they paint?

(A) 10

(B) 14

(C) 20

(D) 28

31. Gavin swims at an average rate of 2 laps per 3 minutes. If he swims for a total of 4 hours over the course of the week, how many laps did he swim?

(A) 40

(B) 80

(C) 120

(D) 160

32. Evaluate: $3 \times 6 \div 2 + 1$.

(A) 9

(B) 10

(C) 11

(D) 12

33. A triangle is inscribed inside of a square. What is the area of the shaded region?

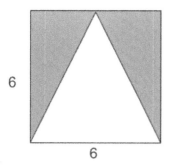

6

6

(A) 9

(B) 18

(C) 24

(D) 36

34. It is currently – 2°C A team cannot play until the temperature reaches 16°C. By approximately how many degrees must the temperature increase before the team can play?

(A) 14

(B) 16

(C) 18

(D) 21

35. The figure shows the first four elements of a dot pattern.

What is the fifth element of this pattern?

(A)

(B)

(C)

(D)

36. In the figure, two equivalent circles are inscribed in a rectangle. What is the area of one circle?

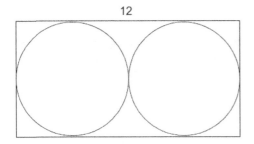

12

(A) 3π

(B) 9π

(C) 18π

(D) 36π

37. A bag has 12 candies that are all the same size: 4 are red, 3 are green, and 5 are blue. What is the probability of choosing a red candy or a green candy?

(A) 1/12

(B) 5/12

(C) 7/12

(D) 11/12

38. Which of the following is equivalent to the expression: $\frac{a}{b}\left(\frac{b}{a} - \frac{b}{2a^2}\right)$

(A) $\frac{b}{a}\left(\frac{a}{b} - \frac{b}{2a^2}\right)$

(B) $\frac{1-ab}{2a^2b}$

(C) $1 - \frac{1}{2a}$

(D) $1 - \frac{1}{2b}$

39. Arthur is drawing a rectangle. Where should he put the last vertex?

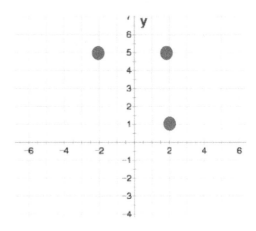

(A) (-2, -1)

(B) (-2, 1)

(C) (-1, -2)

(D) (1, -2)

40. Which of the following numbers is divisible by 3?

(A) 582

(B) 584

(C) 587

(D) 595

41. Which of the following could be a value of x i $4x - 3 < 5$?

(A) 1

(B) 2

(C) 3

(D) 4

42. For which function does the y value decrease at the greatest rate as the x value increases?

(A)

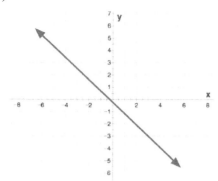

(B)

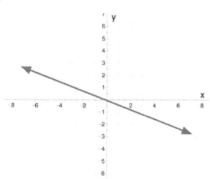

(C)

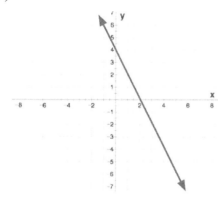

(D)

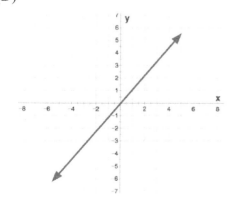

43. Which of the following is equivalent to this expression: $\sqrt{16}(\sqrt{121} + 3x)$

(A) $44 + 3x$

(B) $4\,(11 + 3x)$

(C) $\sqrt{137 + 3x}$

(D) $\sqrt{44} + 3x$

44. What is the slope of the line perpendicular to the line: $3y - 4 = -1x$

(A) -1/3

(B) 1/3

(C) 3

(D) -3

45. Kaila scored an average of 4 points in the first 3 soccer games. How many points does she need to score in the next game to make her average 5 points?

(A) 5

(B) 6

(C) 7

(D) 8

46. The surface area of a cube is 96 ft². What is the volume of the cube?

(A) 32

(B) 64

(C) 96

(D) 108

47. What is the greatest common factor of 35 and 84?

(A) 4

(B) 5

(C) 7

(D) 12

Mathematics Achievement Section – Answers

1. C	17. A	33. B
2. B	18. C	34. C
3. B	19. C	35. A
4. C	20. A	36. B
5. D	21. B	37. C
6. B	22. C	38. C
7. C	23. B	39. B
8. B	24. B	40. A
9. D	25. C	41. A
10. B	26. A	42. C
11. B	27. C	43. B
12. C	28. C	44. C
13. B	29. C	45. D
14. D	30. D	46. B
15. B	31. D	47. C
16. C	32. B	

Scoring your Mathematics Achievement Section

Use this chart to approximate your percentile score based on your number of correct answers.

Applying to 7th Grade:

Correct Answers	19-20	26-27	32-33
Percentile	25th	50th	75th

Applying to 8th Grade:

Correct Answers	21-22	28- 29	35-36
Percentile	25th	50th	75th

A general rule of thumb to calculate your approximate stanine score is to take your # of correct answers and divide by 47. The number in the 10s digit of your percentage score is your approximate stanine score. This isn't a perfect rule, but it can be pretty accurate for the math sections

Percentile ——Stanine

1-3 —— 1

4-10——2

11-22——3

23-39——4

40-59——5

60-76——6

77-88——7

89-95——8

96-99——9

Visit us online!

Go to LarchmontAcademics.com to sign up for our self-paced online ISEE course.

This course will help you prepare for all test section with video lessons and hundreds of targeted practice problems.

Made in the USA
Las Vegas, NV
07 November 2024

11306651R00118